# The Tragedy of
# Julius Caesar

# Hayden Shakespeare Series

Editors:

MAYNARD MACK
Sterling Professor of English, Yale University

ROBERT W. BOYNTON
Former Principal, Senior High School,
and Chairman, English Department, Germantown Friends School

The Tragedy of Hamlet
The Tragedy of Macbeth
The Tragedy of Julius Caesar
The First Part of King Henry the Fourth
The Tragedy of Romeo and Juliet
The Tragedy of Othello, the Moor of Venice
The Life of Henry V
A Midsummer Night's Dream

# The Tragedy of
# Julius Caesar

by William Shakespeare

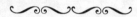

Edited by

Maynard Mack and Robert W. Boynton

HAYDEN BOOK COMPANY, INC., NEW YORK

The figure "The Globe Playhouse, 1599-1613, a Conjectural Reconstruction" is reprinted by permission of Coward-McCann, Inc., from *The Globe Restored: A Study of the Elizabethan Theatre,* Second Edition, by C. Walter Hodges. Copyright © 1953 and 1968 by C. Walter Hodges.

*ISBN 0-8104-6014-9*
*Library of Congress Catalog Card Number 72-88227*
*Copyright © 1973*
HAYDEN BOOK COMPANY, INC. All rights reserved. No part of this book may be reprinted, or reproduced, or utilized in any form or by any electronic, mechanical, or other means, now known or hereafter invented, including photocopying and recording, or in any information storage and retrieval system, without permission in writing from the Publisher.

*Printed in the United States of America*

1  2  3  4  5  6  7  8  9  PRINTING

73 74 75 76 77 78  YEAR

# PREFACE

The Hayden Shakespeare Series offers the Shakespeare plays most widely studied in schools and colleges, in a format designed to be read more easily than the normal pocket-sized editions, yet inexpensive, durable, and, more important, informed by the best in modern Shakespeare scholarship. The plays included in this series are judiciously framed with supporting material, enabling the reader to deal creatively with the text in the classroom, in small groups, or independently.

The editors of this series have founded their work on the following principles:

(1) Reading Shakespeare is not a poor substitute for seeing Shakespeare well performed, but rather a different arena of experience with its own demands and rewards.

(2) Seeing and hearing the language of the play in the theater of the mind is central to the experience the playwright provides.

(3) Knowing something of the characteristics of Shakespeare's own theater lessens the danger of asking the wrong questions about the structure and meaning of his plays.

(4) The text should be as faithful as possible to the most authoritative early edition, with a minimum of editorial interpolation.

(5) Notes and glosses should explain and not simply suggest, but at the same time the reader should be granted his common sense and his mother wit.

(6) Commentary before and after the play does not detract from direct experience—is not intrusive—if it suggests ways of approaching the text that allow the reader a broader range of imaginative involvement.

(7) Questions on the text provoke further questions and provide deepened insight if they are not used or thought of as prodding or testing devices.

Each volume in the series contains an introductory essay which briefly puts the play in its historical context (not because our interest is in theatrical history, but because the play *has* a historical context) and discusses the play's themes and concerns and how Shakespeare went about dramatizing them. Along with the introductory essay is a brief note about the Elizabethan theater, a conjectural reconstruction of the Globe Playhouse, and a general note on the policy of this series with respect to texts, with specific reference to the play in hand.

Following the text there is a commentary on how to approach the play as a live dramatic experience in the theater of the mind. Observations on the imaginative world of the play in general lead into discussions of selected scenes, the intention being to place the sometimes narrow interests of academic Shakespeare study in a context that gives scope to the whole personality of teacher and student and calls up sense and feeling as well as idea and theme.

Also included in the material following the text are questions, specific and general, on the play, some brief information about Shakespeare himself, a chronological listing of his works, and suggested basic reference books, recordings, and films.

The editors would like to thank Francis R. Olley of St. Joseph's College, Philadelphia, for developing the "In the Theater of the Mind" essay for this volume.

# CONTENTS

# INTRODUCTION

*i*

Assassination is at the core of the action in *Julius Caesar*, and its shock waves echo before and after. But you cannot make literature out of the details of killing, no matter how bloody and graphic, even if dozens of films and TV dramas say that you can. The question has to be, what does killing—undertaken for whatever reasons—do to a man and to the world he lives in? Particularly, what does it do to a man of great gifts who kills for what he, and others, consider a great cause, a cause that (for him at least) is truly other-centered more than self-centered? In *Julius Caesar* we have such a man in Brutus. He is not a megalomaniacal assassin, but one of Rome's best citizens, and his tragedy is almost unbearable because it gives an aura of nobility to self-delusion and chisels *"Et tu, Brutè"* on any sane man's heart. There is no better antidote against political or moral self-righteousness, however well-meaning, than a thoughtful reading of *Julius Caesar*.

Caesar is assassinated because certain leading citizens of Rome have convinced themselves, for various reasons, that he is about to take upon himself dictatorial powers. At stake, as they see it, is their future as free men or vassals. At stake, as those loyal to Caesar see it—since he denies that he has any ambition to be dictator—is stability in Rome as against renewed civil chaos. What takes the murder and its consequences out of the realm of sensationalism, of atrocity for atrocity's sake, is Shakespeare's concern for the larger issues that lie behind it, and indeed lie in some degree behind all deliberate taking of life or any deliberate act at all. The play dramatizes the inability

1

of men to direct themselves or even know themselves: the insufficiency of their good intentions and noble aims, for history is also consequences; the insufficiency of their "reasons" and rational expectations, for the ultimate consequences of an act are unpredictable, and usually, by all human standards, illogical as well; and finally, the insufficiency of the human will itself, for there is always something to be reckoned with that is non-human and inscrutable, be it Nemesis, the Fates, Providence, Determinism—men have many names for it, but it is always there.

How do we get these observations out of the bare story of an assassination that breeds the tyranny it is intended to destroy? We get them through the way in which Shakespeare shapes the conflict between the assassins and their victim, through his concern for those on the periphery who are affected by the conflict and in turn affect it, through the intricate arrangement of contrasting episodes.

## *ii*

Let us now look at the play itself, starting with I ii where most of the action is already implicit. We have just learned from I i of Caesar's return in triumph from warring on Pompey's sons, and have seen the warm, though fickle, adulation of the crowd and the apprehension of the tribunes. Now we are to see the great man himself. The procession enters to triumphal music with the hubbub of a great press of people, with young men stripped for the ceremonial races, among them Antony, with statesmen in their togas (Decius, Cicero, Brutus, Cassius, Casca), with the two wives, Calphurnia and Portia, and, in the lead, for not even Calphurnia is permitted at his side, the great man. As he starts to speak, an expectant hush settles over the gathering: what does the great man have on his mind?

> CAESAR.   Calphurnia.
> CASCA.   Peace, ho! Caesar speaks.
> CAESAR.   Calphurnia.
> CALPHURNIA.   Here, my lord.
> CAESAR.   Stand you directly in Antonius' way
>     When he doth run his course. Antonius.
> ANTONY.   Caesar, my lord?

CAESAR.   Forget not in your speed, Antonius,
> To touch Calphurnia; for our elders say
> The barren, touchèd in this holy chase,
> Shake off their sterile curse.

ANTONY.   I shall remember.
> When Caesar says "Do this," it is performed.

(I ii 1-13)

What the great man had on his mind, it appears, was to remind his wife, in this public place, that she is sterile; that there is an old tradition about how sterility can be removed; and that while of course he is much too sophisticated to accept such a superstition himself—it is "our elders" who say it—still, Calphurnia had jolly well better get out there and get tagged, or else!

Then the procession takes up again. The hubbub is resumed, but once more the expectant silence settles as a voice is heard.

SOOTHSAYER.   Caesar!

CAESAR.   Ha! Who calls?

CASCA.   Bid every noise be still. Peace yet again!

CAESAR.   Who is it in the press that calls on me?
> I hear a tongue shriller than all the music
> Cry "Caesar!" Speak. Caesar is turned to hear.

SOOTHSAYER.   Beware the ides of March.

CAESAR.   What man is that?

BRUTUS.   A soothsayer bids you beware the ides of March.

CAESAR.   Set him before me; let me see his face.

CASSIUS.   Fellow, come from the throng; look upon Caesar.

CAESAR.   What say'st thou to me now? Speak once again.

SOOTHSAYER.   Beware the ides of March.

CAESAR.   He is a dreamer. Let us leave him. Pass.

(I ii 15-28)

It is easy to see from these small instances how a first-rate dramatic imagination works. There is no hint of any procession in Plutarch, Shakespeare's source. "Caesar," says Plutarch, "*sat* to behold." There is no mention of Calphurnia in Plutarch's account of the Lupercalian race, and there is no mention anywhere of her sterility. Shakespeare, in nine lines, has given us an unforgettable picture of a man who would like to be emperor pathetically concerned that he lacks an heir, and

determined, even at the cost of making his wife a public spectacle, to establish that this is owing to no lack of virility in him.
The first episode thus dramatizes instantaneously the oncoming
theme of the play: that a man's will is not enough; that there
are other matters to be reckoned with, like the infertility of
one's wife, or one's own affliction of the falling sickness which
spoils everything one hoped for just at the instant when one had
it almost in one's hand. Brutus will be obliged to learn this
lesson too.

In the second episode, the theme develops. We see again
the uneasy rationalism that everybody in this play affects; we
hear it reverberate in the faint contempt—almost a challenge—
of Brutus's words as he turns to Caesar: "A soothsayer bids you
beware the ides of March." Yet underneath, in the soothsayer's
presence and his sober warning, Shakespeare allows us to catch
a hint of something else, something far more primitive and
mysterious, from which rationalism in this play keeps trying
vainly to cut itself away: "He is a dreamer. Let us leave him.
Pass." Only we in the audience are in a position to see that the
dreamer has foretold the path down which all these reasoners
will go to that fatal encounter at the Capitol.

Meantime, in these same two episodes, we have learned
something about the character of Caesar. In the first, it was the
Caesar of human frailties who spoke to us, the husband with
his hopeful superstition. In the second, it was the marble superman of state, impassive, impervious, speaking of himself in the
third person: "Speak! Caesar is turned to hear." He even has
the soothsayer brought before his face to repeat the message, as
if he thought that somehow, in awe of the marble presence, the
message would falter and dissolve: how can a superman need
to beware the ides of March?

We hardly have time to do more than glimpse here a man
of divided selves, when he is gone. But in his absence, the words
of Cassius confirm our glimpse. Cassius's description of him
exhibits the same duality that we had noticed earlier. On the
one hand, an extremely ordinary man whose stamina in the
swimming match was soon exhausted, who, when he had a fever
once in Spain, shook and groaned like a sick girl, who even
now, as we soon learn, is falling down with epilepsy in the
marketplace. On the other hand, a being who has somehow
become a god, who "bears the palm alone," who "bestrides the

narrow world like a Colossus." When the procession returns, no longer festive, but angry and tense, there is the same effect once more. Our one Caesar shows a normal man's suspicion of his enemies, voices some shrewd human observations about Cassius and says to Antony, "Come on my right hand, for this ear is deaf" (I ii 225). Our other Caesar says, as if he were suddenly reminded of something he had forgotten, "I rather tell thee what is to be feared/Than what I fear; for always I am Caesar" (I ii 223-24).

Whenever Caesar appears hereafter, we shall find this singular division in him, and nowhere more so than in the scene in which he receives the conspirators at his house. Some aspects of this scene seem calculated for nothing else than to fix upon our minds the superman conception, the Big Brother of Orwell's *Nineteen Eighty-Four*, the great resonant name echoing down the halls of time. Thus at the beginning of the scene:

> . . . The things that threatened me
> Ne'er looked but on my back. When they shall see
> The face of Caesar, they are vanishèd. (II ii 11-13)

And again later:

> . . . Danger knows full well
> That Caesar is more dangerous than he.
> We are two lions littered in one day,
> And I the elder and more terrible, . . . (II ii 47-50)

And again still later: "Shall Caesar send a lie?" (II ii 70) And again: "The cause is in my will: I will not come." (II ii 76) Other aspects, including his concern about Calphurnia's dream, his vacillation about going to the senate house, and his anxiety about the portents of the night, plainly mark out his human weaknesses. Finally, as is the habit in this Rome, he puts the irrational from him that his wife's intuitions and her dream embody; he accepts the rationalization of the irrational that Decius skillfully manufactures, and, as earlier at the Lupercalia, hides from himself his own vivid sense of forces that lie beyond the will's control by attributing it to her:

> How foolish do your fears seem now, Calphurnia!
> I am ashamèd I did yield to them.
> Give me my robe, for I will go. (II ii 110-12)

*iii*

So far in our consideration of the implications of I ii, we have been looking only at Caesar, the title personage of the play, and its historical center. It is time now to turn to Brutus, the play's tragic center, whom we also find to be a divided man—"poor Brutus," to use his own phrase, "with himself at war." (I ii 51) The war, we realize as the scene progresses, is a conflict between a quiet, essentially domestic and loving nature, and a powerful integrity expressing itself in a sense of honorable duty to the commonweal. This duality in Brutus seems to be what Cassius is probing at in his long disquisition about the mirror. The Brutus looking into the glass that Cassius figuratively holds up to him, the Brutus of this moment, now, in Rome, is a grave, studious, private man, of a wonderfully gentle temper, as we shall see again and again later on, very slow to passion, as Cassius's ill-concealed disappointment in having failed to kindle him to immediate response reveals, a man whose sensitive nature recoils at the hint of violence lurking in some of Cassius's speeches, just as he has already recoiled at going on with Caesar to the marketplace, to witness the mass hysteria of clapping hands, sweaty nightcaps, and stinking breath. This is the present self that looks into Cassius's mirror.

The image that looks back out, that Cassius wants him to see, the potential Brutus, is the man of public spirit, worried already by the question of Caesar's intentions, the lineal descendant of an earlier Brutus who drove a would-be monarch from the city, a man whose body is visibly stiffening in our sight at each huzza from the Forum, and whose anxiety, though he makes no reply to Cassius's inflammatory language, keeps bursting to the surface: "What means this shouting?/I do fear, the people choose Caesar/For their king." (I ii 87-89) The problem at the tragic center of the play, we begin to sense, is to be the tug of private versus public, the individual versus a world he never made, any citizen anywhere versus the selective service greetings that history is always mailing out to each of us. And this problem is to be traversed by that other tug this scene presents, of the irrational versus the rational, the destiny we think we can control versus the destiny that sweeps all before it.

Through I ii, Brutus's public self, the self that responds to these selective service greetings, is no more than a reflection in a mirror, a mere anxiety in his own brain, about which he refuses to confide, even to Cassius. In II i, we see the public self making further headway. First, there is Brutus's argument with himself about the threat of Caesar, and in his conclusion that Caesar must be killed we note how far his private self—he is, after all, one of Caesar's closest friends—has been invaded by the self of public spirit. From here on, the course of the invasion accelerates. The letter comes, tossed from the public world into the private world, into Brutus's garden, and addressing, as Cassius had, that public image reflected in the mirror: "Brutus, thou sleep'st. Awake, and see thyself!" (II i 46) Then follows the well-known brief soliloquy, showing us that Brutus's mind has moved on now from the phase of decision to the inquietudes that follow decision:

> Between the acting of a dreadful thing
> And the first motion, all the interim is
> Like a phantasma or a hideous dream.  (II i 63-65)

What is important to observe is that these lines stress once again the gulf that separates motive from action, that which is interior in man and controllable by his will from that which, once acted, becomes independent of him and moves with a life of its own. This gulf is a no man's land, a phantasma, a hideous dream.

Finally, there arrives in such a form that no audience can miss it the actual visible invasion itself, as this peaceful garden quiet is broken in on by knocking, like the knocking of fate in Beethoven's fifth symphony, and by men with faces hidden in their cloaks. Following this, a lovely interlude with Portia serves to emphasize how much the private self, the private world has been shattered. We have something close to discord here—as much of a discord as these very gentle people are capable of— and though there is a reconciliation at the end and Brutus's promise to confide in her soon, this division in the family is an omen. So is that knock of the latecomer, Caius Ligarius, which reminds us once again of the intrusions of the public life. And when Ligarius throws off his sick man's kerchief on learning that there is an honorable exploit afoot, we may see in it an epitome of the whole scene, a graphic visual renunciation, like

Brutus's, of the private good to the public; and we may see this also in Brutus's own exit a few lines later, not into the inner house where Portia waits for him, but out into the thunder and lightning of the public life of Rome. It is perhaps significant that at our final view of Portia, two scenes later, she too stands outside the privacy of the house, her mind wholly occupied with thoughts of what is happening at the Capitol, and trying to put on a public self for Brutus's sake: "Run, Lucius, and commend me to my lord;/ Say I am merry. . . ." (II iv 49-50)

Meantime, up there by the Capitol, the tragic center and the historical center meet. The suspense is very great as Caesar, seeing the Soothsayer in the throng, reminds him that the ides of March are come, and receives in answer, "Ay, Caesar, but not gone" (III i 2). More suspense as Artemidorus presses forward with the paper that we know contains a full discovery of the plot. Decius, apprehensive, steps quickly into the breach with another paper, a petition from Trebonius. More suspense still as Popilius sidles past Cassius with the whisper, "I wish your enterprise to-day may thrive," (III i 14) and then moves on to Caesar's side, where he engages him in animated talk. But they detect no telltale change in Caesar's countenance; Trebonius steps into his assignment and takes Antony aside; Metellus Cimber throws himself at Caesar's feet; Brutus gives the signal to "press near and second him," and Caesar's "Are we all ready?" draws every eye to Caesar's chair. One by one they all kneel before this demigod—an effective tableau which gives a coloring of priest-like ritual to what they are about to do. Caesar is to bleed, but, as Brutus has said, they will sublimate the act into a sacrifice:

> Let's kill him boldly, but not wrathfully;
> Let's carve him as a dish fit for the gods,
> Not hew him as a carcass fit for hounds. (II i 179-81)

Everything in the scene must underscore this ceremonial attitude, in order to bring out the almost fatuous cleavage between Brutus's self-deception about the spirit of this enterprise and its bloody purpose.

The Caesar that we are permitted to see while all this ceremony is preparing is almost entirely the superman, for obvious reasons. To give a color of justice to Brutus's act and so to preserve our sense of his nobility even if we happen to think the assassination a mistake, as an Elizabethan audience emphatically would, Caesar has to appear in a mood of superhumanity at least as fatuous as the conspirators' mood of sacrifice. Hence Shakespeare makes him first of all insult Metellus Cimber: "If thou dost bend and pray and fawn for him,/I spurn thee like a cur" (III i 49-50); then comment with intolerable pomposity, and, in fact, blasphemy, on his own iron resolution, for he affects to be immovable even by prayer and hence superior to the very gods. Finally, Shakespeare puts into his mouth one of those supreme arrogances that will remind us of the destroying *hubris* which makes men mad in order to ruin them. "Hence!" Caesar cries, "Wilt thou lift up Olympus?" (III i 80) It is at just this point, when the colossus Caesar drunk with self-love is before us, that Casca strikes. Then they all strike, with a last blow that brings out for the final time the other, human side of this double Caesar: "Et tu, Brutè?"

And now this little group of men has altered history. The representative of the evil direction it was taking toward autocratic power lies dead before them. The direction to which it must be restored becomes emphatic in Cassius's cry of "Liberty, freedom, and enfranchisement!" Solemnly, and again like priests who have just sacrificed a victim, they kneel together and bathe their hands and swords in Caesar's blood. Brutus explains:

> Then walk we forth, even to the market place,
> And waving our red weapons o'er our heads,
> Let's all cry "Peace, freedom, and liberty!" (III i 118-20)

If the conjunction of those red hands and weapons with this slogan is not enough to bring an audience up with a start, the next passage will be, for now the conspirators explicitly invoke the judgment of history on their deed. On the stages of theaters the world over, so they anticipate, this lofty incident will be re-enacted, and

> So oft as that shall be,
> So often shall the knot of us be called
> The men that gave their country liberty. (III i 127-29)

We, the audience, recalling what actually did result in Rome— the civil wars, the long line of despotic emperors—cannot miss the irony of their prediction, an irony that insists on our recognizing that this effort to control history is going to fail. Why does it fail?

*iv*

One reason why is shown us in the next few moments. The leader of this assault on history is, like many another reformer, a man of high idealism, who devoutly believes that the rest of the world is like himself. It was just to kill Caesar— so he persuades himself—because he was a great threat to freedom. It would not have been just to kill Antony, and he vetoed the idea. Even now, when the consequence of that decision has come back to face him in the shape of Antony's servant, kneeling before him, he sees no reason to reconsider it. There are good grounds for what they have done, he says; Antony will hear them, and be satisfied. With Antony, who shortly arrives in person, he takes this line again:

> Our reasons are so full of good regard
> That were you, Antony, the son of Caesar,
> You should be satisfied. (III i 240-42)

With equal confidence in the rationality of man, he puts by Cassius's fears of what Antony will do if allowed to address the people: "By your pardon;/I will myself into the pulpit first/ And show the reason of our Caesar's death." (III i 254-56) Here is a man so much a friend of Caesar's that he is still speaking of him as "our Caesar," so capable of rising to what he takes to be his duty that he has taken on the leadership of those who intend to kill him, so trusting of common decency that he expects the populace will respond to reason, and Antony to the obligation laid on him by their permitting him to speak. At such a man, one hardly knows whether to laugh or cry.

The same mixture of feelings is likely to be stirring in us as Brutus speaks to the people in III ii. This is a speech in what used to be called the great liberal tradition, the tradition that assumed, as our American founding fathers did, that men in the mass are reasonable. It has therefore been made a prose oration, spare and terse in diction, tightly patterned in syntax so that it requires close attention, and founded, with respect to its argument, on three elements: the abstract sentiment of duty to the state (because he endangered Rome, Caesar had to be slain); the abstract sentiment of political justice (because he was ambitious, Caesar deserved his fall); and the moral authority of the man Brutus. As long as that moral authority is concretely before them in Brutus's presence, the populace is impressed. But since they are not trained minds, and only trained minds respond accurately to abstractions, they do not understand the content of his argument at all, as one of them indicates by shouting, "Let him be Caesar!" What moves them is the obvious sincerity and the known integrity of the speaker; and when he finishes, they are ready to carry him off on their shoulders on that account alone, leaving Antony a vacant Forum. The fair-mindedness of Brutus is thrilling but painful to behold as he calms this triumphal surge in his favor, urges them to stay and hear Antony, and then, in a moment very impressive dramatically as well as symbolically, walks off the stage, alone. We see then, if we have not seen before, the first answer to the question why the attack on history failed. It was blinded, as it so often has been, by the very idealism that impelled it.

When Antony takes the rostrum, we begin to get a second answer. It has been said by somebody that in a school for demagogues this speech should be the whole curriculum. Antony himself describes its method when he observes in the preceding scene, apropos of the effect of Caesar's dead body on the messenger from Octavius, "Passion, I see, is catching" (III i 303). This is a statement that cannot be made about reason.

Because of his known integrity, Brutus formulates from the outset, on no other authority than his own, positive propositions about Caesar and about his own motives. Antony takes the safer alternative of concealing propositions in questions, by which the audience's mind is then guided to conclusions which seem its own:

> He hath brought many captives home to Rome,
> Whose ransoms did the general coffers fill.
> Did this in Caesar seem ambitious? (III ii 95-97)

> You all did see that on the Lupercal
> I thrice presented him a kingly crown,
> Which he did thrice refuse. Was this ambition?
> (III ii 102-104)

How well Shakespeare knew his crowds can be seen in the replies to Antony. Brutus, appealing to their reason, was greeted with wild outbursts of uncomprehending emotion: "Let him be Caesar!" Antony appeals only to their emotions and their pockets, but now they say, "Methinks there is much reason in his sayings," and chew upon it seriously.

Second, Antony stirs up impulses and then thwarts them. He appeals to their curiosity and their greed in the matter of the will, but then he doesn't come clean on it. In the same manner, he stirs up their rage against the conspirators, yet always pretends to hold them back: "I fear I wrong the honorable men/Whose daggers have stabbed Caesar; I do fear it" (III ii 158-59). Third, and this is largely the technical means by which he accomplishes the stirring up, his speech is baited with irony. The passage just quoted is a typical specimen. So is the famous refrain, "For Brutus is an honorable man." Now the rhetorical value of irony is that it stimulates the mind to formulate the contrary, that is, the intended meaning. It stimulates what the psychologists of propaganda nowadays call the assertive factor. "Are you the one man in seven who shaves daily?" "Did your husband forget to kiss you this morning?" The advertiser's technique is not, of course, ironical, but it illustrates the effect.

Finally, Antony rests his case, not, like Brutus, on abstractions centering in the state and political justice, but on emotions centering in the individual listener. The first great crescendo of the speech, which culminates in the passage on Caesar's wounds, appeals first to pity and then to indignation. The second one, culminating in the reading of Caesar's will, appeals first to curiosity and greed and then to gratitude. The management of the will is particularly cunning: it is an item more concrete than any words could be, an actual tantalizing document that can be flashed before the eye. It is described, at first vaguely, as being of such a sort that they would honor Caesar for it. Then, closer to home, as something which would show "how Caesar loved you." Then, with an undisguised appeal to self-interest, as a testament that will make them his "heirs." The emotions aroused by this news enable Antony to make a final test of his ironical refrain about the "honorable men," and finding the results all that he had hoped, he can come down now among the crowd as one of them, and appeal directly to their feelings by appealing to his own: "If you have tears, prepare to shed them now" (III ii 176).

The success of this direct appeal to passion can be seen at its close. Where formerly we had a populace, now we have a mob. Since it is a mob, its mind can be sealed against any later seepage of rationality back into it by the insinuation that reasoning is always false anyway—simply a surface covering up private grudges, like the "reason" they have heard from Brutus; whereas from Antony himself, the plain blunt friend of Caesar, they are getting the plain blunt truth and (a favorite trick of politicians) only what they already know to be the truth.

But also, since it is a mob and therefore will eventually cool off, it must be called back one final time to hear the will. Antony no longer needs this as an incentive to riot; the mingled rage and pity he has aroused will take care of that. But when the hangover comes, and you are remembering how that fellow looked swaying a little on the rope's end, with his eyes bugging out and the veins knotted at his temples, then it is good to have something really reasonable to cling to, like seventy-five drachmas (or even thirty pieces of silver) and some orchards along a river.

At about this point, it becomes impossible not to see that a second reason for the failure of the attack on history is what it left out of account—what all these Romans from the beginning, except Antony, have been trying to leave out of account: the phenomenon of feeling, the nonrational factor in men, in the world, in history itself—of which this blind infuriated mob is one kind of exemplification. Too secure in his own fancied suppression of the subrational, Brutus has failed altogether to reckon with its power. Thus he could seriously say to Antony in the passage quoted earlier: Antony, even if you were "the son of Caesar/You should be satisfied," as if the feeling of a son for a murdered father could ever be "satisfied" by reasons. And thus, too, he could walk off the stage alone, urging the crowd to hear Antony, the very figure of embodied "reason," unaware that only the irrational is catching.

Meantime, the scene of the mob tearing Cinna the Poet to pieces simply for having the same name as one of the conspirators (III iii) gives us our first taste of the chaos invoked by Antony when he stood alone over Caesar's corpse. And as we consider that prediction and this mob, we are bound to realize that there is a third reason why the attack on history failed. As we have seen already, history is only partly responsive to noble motives, only partly responsive to rationality. Now we see —what Shakespeare hinted in the beginning with those two episodes of Calphurnia and the soothsayer—that it is only partly responsible to human influence of any sort. With all their reasons, the conspirators and Caesar only carried out what the soothsayer foreknew. There is, in short, a determination in history, whether we call it natural or providential, which at least *helps* to shape our ends, "rough hew them how we will." One of the names of that factor in this play is Caesarism. Brutus put the point, all unconsciously, in that scene when the conspirators were gathered at his house. He said:

> We all stand up against the spirit of Caesar,
> And in the spirit of men there is no blood.
> O that we then could come by Caesar's spirit
> And not dismember Caesar! But, alas,
> Caesar must bleed for it! (II i 174-78)

Then Caesar did bleed for it, but his spirit, as Brutus's own remark should have told him, proved to be invulnerable. It was only set free by his assassination, and now, as Antony says, "ranging for revenge, . . . Shall in these confines with a monarch's voice/Cry 'Havoc' and let slip the dogs of war" (III i 290-93).

It is clear all through Acts IV and V that Brutus and Cassius are defeated before they begin to fight. Antony knows it and says so at V i. Cassius knows it too. Cassius, an Epicurean in philosophy, and therefore one who has never heretofore believed in omens, now mistrusts his former rationalism: he suspects there may be something after all in those ravens, crows, and kites that wheel overhead. Brutus too mistrusts *his* rationalism. As a Stoic, his philosophy requires him to repudiate suicide, but he admits to Cassius that if the need comes he will repudiate philosophy instead. This, like Cassius's statement, is an unconscious admission of the force of unreason in human affairs, an unreason that makes its presence felt again and again during the great battle. Cassius, for instance, fails to realize that Octavius "Is overthrown by noble Brutus's power," becomes the victim of a mistaken report of Titinius's death, runs on his sword crying, "Caesar, thou art revenged," and is greeted, dead, by Brutus, in words that make still clearer their defeat by history: "O Julius Caesar, thou art mighty yet!/Thy spirit walks abroad and turns our swords/In our own proper entrails" (V iii 99-101). In the same vein, when it is Brutus's turn to die, we learn that the ghost of Caesar has reappeared, and he thrusts the sword home, saying, "Caesar, now be still" (V v 56).

*v*

In summary, then, Shakespeare's theme in *Julius Caesar* has to do with the always ambiguous impact between man and history. During the first half of the play, what we are chiefly conscious of is the human will as a force in history—men making choices, controlling events. Our typical scenes are I ii, where a man is trying to make up his mind; or II i, where a man first reaches a decision and then, with his fellows, lays plans to implement it; or II ii, where we have Decius Brutus persuading Caesar to decide to go to the senate house; or III i and ii, where up through the assassination, and even up through Antony's speech, men are still, so to speak, impinging on history, molding it to their conscious will.

But then comes a change. Though we still have men in action trying to mold their world, one senses a real shift in the direction of the impact. In the second half of the play, our typical scenes are those like III iii, where Antony has raised something that is no longer under his control; or like IV i, where we see men acting as if (under the control of expediency or necessity or call it what you will) they no longer had wills of their own, but prick down the names of nephews and brothers indiscriminately for slaughter; or like IV iii and all the scenes thereafter, where we are constantly made to feel that Cassius and Brutus are in the hands of something bigger than they know.

In this light, we can readily see why Shakespeare gave Caesar and Brutus double characters, public-private selves. The public Caesar, that marble man, that everlasting Big Brother, is a constant dehumanizing threat to everyone else and must in some way be eliminated, exorcised, dispatched, over and over again because he never dies. The private Caesar, who has human ailments and is a human friend, can be killed once and for all. The private Brutus, that passionate Stoic, that paragon of reason, compassion, self-possession, honor, reputation— "this," as Antony says, "was a man." The public Brutus, who *must* act when duty calls, who must strike marble in his turn, expects everything but the self-destroying realization that a noble cause can never be served by ignoble means.

Who among us is not cursed with the same ingrained contradictions? Who among us is not potentially Caesar or Brutus? Every nation, family, classroom is potentially so much a Rome that there is no reason to see in Shakespeare's play only a piece of ancient history.

A Note on the Elizabethan Theater

Most present-day productions of Elizabethan plays use sets designed to provide a single flexible and suggestive background against which their multiple scenes can flow easily one into the next. Elizabethan plays have to be staged that way if they are not to be distorted, because that is the way they are built. Though the modern playwright is limited by the nature of his theater to as few changes of locale as possible, his Elizabethan counterpart was encouraged by *his* theater to range the whole world of space and time, because his theater was in fact an image of the world. Shakespeare's own theater was even called the world—i.e., the "Globe."

In today's theaters, for the most part, audience and play are emphatically separate. They are separated physically by the architecture of the theater, which has a drop-curtain, footlights, often an orchestra pit, and always a proscenium arch (the arch covered by the curtain), on one side of which the audience sits hushed in almost total darkness, while on the other side the persons of the play move and talk in spots, or floods, of blazing light.

This physical separation of audience from play is expressive of the figurative gulf which, in our theater, also divides them. For the illusion that the modern theater imposes is that the audience is "not really" present, but is eavesdropping, and that the people it looks in on are "really" men and women going about real business in a real room from which one wall has been removed.

What this means for those on the bright side of the footlights is that everything must be made as completely "present" as actors, scene-painters, and stage-carpenters can manage; it is not enough to suggest reality, it must be simulated. The implication for those on the dark side of the footlights is that they must become as "unpresent" as they can—in other words detached, silent, and passive, like the eavesdroppers they are. Actually, neither of these extremes is ever reached in our theater, or even closely approached, but the tendency of enhanced realism on one side of the curtain to generate passivity on the other has spurred many modern playwrights to search for ways of recapturing the cooperative relation between audience and play that Shakespeare's theater had.

Physically the Globe was a wooden building shaped probably like a polygon outside and circular inside, some thirty or forty feet high, with three tiers of roofed galleries, one on top of the other straight up, opera-house style, around the entire interior. The center of the enclosure (the "pit"), some fifty or so feet in diameter, was unroofed, and into it jutted the raised rectangular stage, fully half the way across the pit and almost forty feet wide. Above part of the stage, as a cover, supported on pillars, was a sloping roof, called the "Heavens," the ceiling of which was brightly painted with stars and other astronomical figures. Below the stage, reached by trap doors, was "Hell." At the rear wall, doors on either side gave access between the stage and the dressing rooms. Toward the rear of the stage there was an "inner" playing area, probably a sort of alcove (but sometimes misleadingly called the "inner stage"), which could be left opened or curtained. Directly above this was an "upper" playing area (the "upper stage"), which probably took the form of a balcony. Above this was another, smaller balcony for the musicians; for the use of music, in tragedy as well as comedy, was one of the conventions of Elizabethan plays.

What scenery there was in theaters like the Globe took chiefly the form of simple props. There was no artificial lighting of any kind in the theater, which meant that performances were always given by daylight—in the afternoon. The interior of the building was handsomely decorated, and the dress of the actors (males only—boys played the female roles) expensive and re-

THE GLOBE PLAYHOUSE, 1599-1613

*A Conjectural Reconstruction*

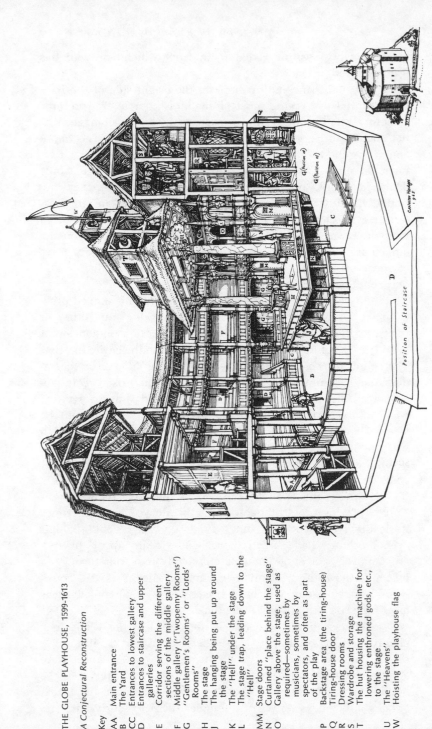

Key

AA  Main entrance
B   The Yard
CC  Entrances to lowest gallery
D   Entrances to staircase and upper
     galleries
E   Corridor serving the different
     sections of the middle gallery
F   Middle gallery ("Twopenny Rooms")
G   "Gentlemen's Rooms" or "Lords'
     Rooms"
H   The stage
J   The hanging being put up around
     the stage
K   The "Hell" under the stage
L   The stage trap, leading down to the
     "Hell"
MM  Stage doors
N   Curtained "place behind the stage"
O   Gallery above the stage, used as
     required—sometimes by
     musicians, sometimes by
     spectators, and often as part
     of the play
P   Backstage area (the tiring-house)
Q   Tiring-house door
R   Dressing rooms
S   Wardrobe and storage
T   The hut housing the machine for
     lowering enthroned gods, etc.,
     to the stage
U   The "Heavens"
W   Hoisting the playhouse flag

splendent, although there was little concern for what we would call authentic period costuming.

The important thing to bear in mind about the Elizabethan theater is that the stage physically dominated the open area and that the audience literally enveloped the actors and the action. As many as two thousand people might be present. Many stood shoulder to shoulder in the pit, surrounding the chest-high open platform on three sides. Behind them in the tiered galleries, at no place more than forty or fifty feet from the stage, sat hundreds of others on benches. In these circumstances, it was easy for the viewers' sense of involvement in the play, and the actors' sense of involvement with the audience before and behind them, to become more intense than in our theater.

The playwright who writes for such a theater as this cannot shape his play as if the audience were not "there": it is irremovably there, every member of it visible to every other in the broad light coming from the open roof. So he necessarily acknowledges its presence, engages its imagination. He feels free, for example, to give his characters "asides"—speeches spoken wholly or mainly for the benefit of the audience, and which those on stage are not supposed to hear. He also gives his characters "soliloquies"—longer speeches by means of which the leading characters may open heart and mind directly to the audience. Further, since his stage is a bare platform without scenery, he calls repeatedly on the imagination of the audience to flesh out the suggestions of hour, place, weather, or mood that he can only communicate to them through the play's own words.

The dramatist who writes for the theater we have been describing has unparalleled opportunities to make the theater audience do duty as an extension, an overflow, an amplification of the very limited stage-audiences which a small company of actors can muster. When, for instance, Shakespeare's Antony addresses the Roman mob in *Julius Caesar*, in a theater where we of the audience surround him on three sides, the realization comes on us increasingly as he speaks that it is we who fill out that tiny group of listeners onstage into the formidable mob he *seems* to harangue; and when King Harry in *Henry V* exhorts his soldiers—"You noblest English"—to battle bravely against the French, we realize (as Shakespeare's own audiences must have done, and in their case with a sharp quickening of the pulse) that it is *we* who are being addressed: *we* are those "noblest English" who are being implored never to yield.

Interactions like these between play and audience are not impossible in the modern theater, but they were a good deal easier to effect in Shakespeare's. Partly, as we have noticed, because of the close physical proximity of audience to player. Partly, as we have also noticed, because the audience's imagination was implicated in the play by the very austerity of a stage without scenery. And partly because the Elizabethan theater's inheritance from the medieval theater (where the stories acted out were primarily Bible stories and therefore "true" in one sense while remaining "stories" in another sense) encouraged an easy traffic back and forth between what was "real" and what was "play."

As has been mentioned, over part of the stage stretched a ceiling called the "Heavens," and under the stage, reached by trap doors through which witches and other apparitions might rise, lay an area called "Hell." And in front of the theater, in the case of Shakespeare's Globe (if we may believe a plausible tradition), was inscribed the legend: *Totus mundus agit histrionem*—"Everybody is an actor"; or, as Shakespeare himself paraphrased it in *As You Like It,* "All the world's a stage, and all the men and women merely players." Thus the individual actor whom the audience saw on the stage playing Julius Caesar or Hamlet or Macbeth was capable of being translated, at any moment, by the very symbolism of that stage, into an image of Every Man working out his human destiny (as the men and women watching him would also have to work out theirs) between the powers of Hell and Heaven.

It is because the characters of Shakespeare were created for a theater like this that they take special hold of us. They have the intensity that comes from believing that the world is a stage, where we are given only our little hour to work out eternal salvation or damnation: and they have the grandeur that comes from believing that the stage is a world, which reaches out past the actors to the theater audience, past them to the audience we call history, past this to the cosmic audience of land, sea, air, moon, sun, and stars (which Elizabethan heroes do not hesitate to address), and so at last to the audience Hamlet turns to when the appearance of the Ghost makes it unmistakable that there are more things in heaven and earth than are dreamed of in human philosophies: "Angels and ministers of grace defend us!"

## Textual Note

Although Shakespeare had no connection with their actual publication, eighteen of his thirty-seven plays were published in various quarto editions before his death in 1616. Not until 1623 were all but one of the plays usually credited to him published in a single volume, now called the First Folio. (A folio is a book made up of sheets folded in half, creating four individual pages per sheet; a quarto is one made up of sheets folded in half and in half again, producing eight pages per sheet.) The First Folio was compiled by two of Shakespeare's actor-colleagues who drew upon the best previous quarto editions of single plays, where available, and on fairly reliable unpublished manuscripts and theater promptbooks. For whatever reason, they omitted from their collection two plays which most scholars today attribute wholly or in part to Shakespeare (*Pericles, Prince of Tyre* and *The Two Noble Kinsmen*) and one play (*Sir Thomas More*) in which it is believed he had a hand.

The policy of the Hayden Shakespeare Series is to use the earliest sound version of each play—either the Folio text or (if one exists) a good quarto text with collations from the Folio—and a minimum of emendation. In lineation, we follow a similarly conservative policy. Most modern editors space the line fragments, with which two successive speeches often end and begin, as a single pentameter line. A case can be made for this procedure, but after considerable reflection we have abandoned it, because we believe that in these situations the lineation of the original editions more often than not throws interesting light on speaking emphasis, pause, and rhythm, and also eliminates a possible reading distraction. We have everywhere normalized and modernized the spelling and punctuation of the original texts, printed character names in full, and added (inconspicuously) act-scene divisions, following the practice of the Globe edition (1864), to which concordances of Shakespeare refer. All matter placed in brackets in the text, including stage directions, is editorial and does not appear in the original version being used.

The line numbering and the act-scene indicators at the top of each page are for convenient reference. The small degree sign (°) indicates a gloss or footnote at the bottom of the page, keyed by line number. The cue phrase is printed in boldface, the gloss or footnote in roman.

The only text of *Julius Caesar* is found in the First Folio. It is a remarkably good text, comparatively free of errors (see, however, IV iii 203-18), and supplied with stage directions that seem to derive from actual theater performance (e.g. "Enter Boy with wine and tapers"). Both circumstances suggest that a playhouse promptbook was its source. We have corrected a few obvious misprints and normalized the Folio's *Antonio, Caska, Claudio, Flavio, Labio, Lucillius, Murellus* (and *Murrellus*), *Octavio,* and *Varrus* into the more usual forms *Antonius, Casca, Claudius, Flavius, Labeo, Lucilius, Marullus, Octavius,* and *Varro.*

# THE TRAGEDY OF
# JULIUS CAESAR

[*Dramatis Personae*

JULIUS CAESAR
OCTAVIUS CAESAR ⎤
MARCUS ANTONIUS ⎬ triumvirs after the death of
M. AEMILIUS LEPIDUS ⎦ Julius Caesar

CICERO ⎤
PUBLIUS ⎬ senators
POPILIUS LENA ⎦

MARCUS BRUTUS ⎤
CASSIUS |
CASCA |
TREBONIUS |
LIGARIUS ⎬ conspirators against Julius Caesar
DECIUS BRUTUS |
METELLUS CIMBER |
CINNA ⎦

FLAVIUS AND MARULLUS, tribunes of the people
ARTEMIDORUS, a teacher of rhetoric
A SOOTHSAYER
CINNA, a poet
ANOTHER POET

LUCILIUS ⎤
TITINIUS |
MESSALA ⎬ friends to Brutus and Cassius
YOUNG CATO |
VOLUMNIUS ⎦

VARRO ⎤
CLITUS |
CLAUDIUS ⎬ servants to Brutus
STRATO |
LUCIUS |
DARDANIUS ⎦

PINDARUS, servant to Cassius
A SERVANT to Caesar; to Anthony; to Octavius
CALPHURNIA, wife to Caesar
PORTIA, wife to Brutus
THE GHOST OF CAESAR
SENATORS, CITIZENS, GUARDS, ATTENDANTS, &C.

*Scene: Rome; near Sardis; near Philippi*]

# The Tragedy of
# Julius Caesar

*Enter Flavius, Marullus, and certain*      I i
*Commoners over the stage.*

FLAVIUS.  Hence! home, you idle creatures, get you home!
Is this a holiday? What, know you not,
Being mechanical,° you ought not walk
Upon a laboring day without the sign°
Of your profession? Speak, what trade° art thou?  5

CARPENTER.  Why, sir, a carpenter.

MARULLUS.  Where is thy leather apron and thy rule?
What dost thou with thy best apparel on?
You, sir, what trade are you?

COBBLER.  Truly, sir, in respect of° a fine workman I am but, 10
as you would say, a cobbler.°

MARULLUS.  But what trade art thou? Answer me directly.°

COBBLER.  A trade, sir, that I hope I may use with a safe con-
science, which is indeed, sir, a mender of bad soles.°

FLAVIUS.  What trade, thou knave? Thou naughty° knave, what 15
trade?

COBBLER.  Nay, I beseech you, sir, be not out° with me. Yet
if you be out,° sir, I can mend° you.

---

I i 3 **Being mechanical** i.e. belonging to
the working class
**4 sign** i.e. working clothes and tools (see
7)
**5 profession, trade** (in Elizabethan usage,
indistinguishable)
**10 in respect of** compared to
**11 cobbler** (1) bungler (Marullus takes it
in this sense) (2) shoe repairer

**12 directly** i.e. without quibbling
**14 soles** (1) soles (2) souls (Flavius, taking it in this second sense, continues to ask
the "bungler's" trade)
**15 naughty** worthless (from "naught")
**16 out** out of humor, angry
**17 out** i.e. out at heel or toe
**17 mend** (1) repair your shoes (2) improve your character (see 13-14)

25

MARULLUS.   What mean'st thou by that? Mend me, thou saucy
    fellow?

COBBLER.   Why, sir, cobble you.

FLAVIUS.   Thou art a cobbler, art thou?                                20

COBBLER.   Truly, sir, all that I live by is with the awl.° I
    meddle with no tradesman's matters nor women's matters;°
    but withal°—I am indeed, sir, a surgeon to old shoes.
    When they are in great danger,° I recover° them. As
    proper° men as ever trod upon neat's leather° have gone 25
    upon my handiwork.

FLAVIUS.   But wherefore art not in thy shop to-day?
    Why dost thou lead these men about the streets?

COBBLER.   Truly, sir, to wear out their shoes, to get myself into
    more work. But indeed,° sir, we make holiday to see Caesar 30
    and to rejoice in his triumph.°

MARULLUS.   Wherefore rejoice?
    What conquest° brings he home?
    What tributaries° follow him to Rome
    To grace in captive bonds his chariot wheels?                    35
    You blocks, you stones, you worse than senseless things!
    O you hard hearts, you cruel men of Rome!
    Knew you not Pompey?° Many a time and oft
    Have you climbed up to walls and battlements,
    To tow'rs and windows, yea, to chimney tops,                     40
    Your infants in your arms, and there have sat
    The livelong day, with patient expectation,
    To see great Pompey pass the streets of Rome.
    And when you saw his chariot but appear,
    Have you not made an universal shout,                            45

---

21 **with the awl** (probably pronounced to
sound like "withal," which recurs in 23)
22 **women's matters** private business (with
a sexual innuendo)
23 **withal** (1) nevertheless (2) with "awl,"
i.e. stiff needle for making holes (3) with
all, i.e. I meddle with all matters (unsaying
what he has just said)
24 **in . . . danger** i.e. ill
24 **recover** (1) heal (2) re-cover (with
leather)
25 **proper** fine, handsome, i.e. his wares
have been worn by the best ("as . . .
leather" is a proverbial phrase)

25 **neat's leather** cowhide
30 **indeed** actually
31 **triumph** i.e. triumphal procession
33 **conquest** Caesar's present victory had
been in a civil war with Romans (the two
sons of his former rival, Cneius Pompeius),
not foreign nations
34 **tributaries** captives, who will pay "tribute" for their release
38 **Pompey** Cneius Pompeius Magnus,
Caesar's fellow triumvir and later rival,
whom he defeated in 48 B.C., and who was
murdered soon after

That° Tiber trembled underneath her banks
To hear the replication° of your sounds
Made in her concave° shores?
And do you now put on your best attire?
And do you now cull out° a holiday?                          50
And do you now strew flowers in his way
That comes in triumph over Pompey's blood?°
Be gone!
Run to your houses, fall upon your knees,
Pray to the gods to intermit° the plague                     55
That needs must light on this ingratitude.

FLAVIUS.  Go, go, good countrymen, and for this fault
Assemble all the poor men of your sort;
Draw them to Tiber banks, and weep your tears
Into the channel, till the lowest stream                     60
Do kiss the most exalted shores of all.°
                              *Exeunt all the Commoners.*
See, whe'r° their basest mettle° be not moved.
They vanish tongue-tied in their guiltiness.
Go you down that way towards the Capitol;
This way will I. Disrobe the images°                         65
If you do find them decked with ceremonies.°

MARULLUS.  May we do so?
You know it is the feast of Lupercal.°

FLAVIUS.  It is no matter. Let no images
Be hung with Caesar's trophies. I'll about°                  70
And drive away the vulgar° from the streets.
So do you too, where you perceive them thick.

---

46  **That** such that
47  **replication** echo
48  **concave** i.e. hollowed out by weather
and water into something resembling an
echo chamber
50  **cull out** pick yourselves out
52  **blood** (1) kin, i.e. his sons (?) (2) all
the blood shed in Pompey's cause (?)
55  **intermit** postpone
**60-61  till . . . all** i.e. till the Tiber floods
—with perhaps the implication that by their
repentant tears they may not only deflect
the gods' anger but rise from baseness (like
"the lowest stream") to be worthy of great
Pompey (The sympathies of Marullus and
Flavius are obviously not with Caesar)

62  **whe'r** whether
62  **their . . . mettle** i.e. even their vulgar
natures
65  **images** i.e. of Caesar
66  **ceremonies** decorations symbolizing his
kinglike power (see I ii 294-95)
68  **Lupercal** February festival of Lupercus,
patron god of farmers and herdsmen; to
"disrobe" Caesar's images at such a time
could appear to be a crime against both
public order (the city's established festival)
and religion (homage to the god)
70  **about** roam about
71  **vulgar** crowd

These growing feathers plucked from Caesar's wing
Will make him fly an ordinary pitch,°
Who else would soar above the view of men°                    75
And keep us all in servile fearfulness.          *Exeunt.*

❧~❧~❧~❧~❧

[*Music.*] *Enter Caesar, Antony (for the course°), Calphurnia,*   I ii
*Portia, Decius, Cicero, Brutus, Cassius, Casca, [a great crowd*
*following, among them] a Soothsayer; after them,*
*Marullus and Flavius.*

CAESAR.   Calphurnia.°

CASCA.   Peace, ho! Caesar speaks.          [*Music ceases.*]

CAESAR.   Calphurnia.

CALPHURNIA.   Here, my lord.

CAESAR.   Stand you directly in Antonius' way                  5
When he doth run his course. Antonius.

ANTONY.   Caesar, my lord?

CAESAR.   Forget not in your speed, Antonius,
To touch Calphurnia; for our elders say
The barren, touchèd in this holy chase,                        10
Shake off their sterile curse.

ANTONY.   I shall remember.
When Caesar says "Do this," it is performed.

CAESAR.   Set on,° and leave no ceremony out.          [*Music.*]

SOOTHSAYER.   Caesar!                                          15

CAESAR.   Ha! Who calls?

CASCA.   Bid every noise be still. Peace yet again! [*Music ceases.*]

---

**73-74 These . . . pitch** Caesar is compared
to a falcon, the height ("pitch") of whose
flight can be controlled by taking feathers
from his wings
**75 soar . . . men** become like a god (an-
ticipating the anxiety that, in I ii, is shared
by Cassius and Brutus)
**I ii s.d. for the course** i.e. he is stripped
to take part in the Lupercalian race, a fer-
tility rite in which young men ran through

the streets brandishing leather thongs while
both pregnant and childless women pressed
forward to be struck, in the belief it would
give them an easy delivery or enable them
to conceive (see 8-12)
**1 Calphurnia** (Shakespeare's spelling
throughout *Julius Caesar* of Plutarch's "Cal-
purnia")
**14 Set on** proceed

CAESAR.   Who is it in the press° that calls on me?
I hear a tongue shriller than all the music
Cry "Caesar!" Speak. Caesar is turned to hear.°       20

SOOTHSAYER.   Beware the ides° of March.

CAESAR.   What man is that?

BRUTUS.   A soothsayer bids you beware the ides of March.

CAESAR.   Set him before me; let me see his face.

CASSIUS.   Fellow, come from the throng; look upon Caesar.    25

CAESAR.   What say'st thou to me now? Speak once again.°

SOOTHSAYER.   Beware the ides of March.

CAESAR.   He is a dreamer. Let us leave him. Pass.
           *Sennet.° Exeunt. Mane[n]t° Brutus and Cassius.*

CASSIUS.   Will you go see the order of the course?°

BRUTUS.   Not I.                                   30

CASSIUS.   I pray you do.

BRUTUS.   I am not gamesome.° I do lack some part
Of that quick° spirit that is in Antony.
Let me not hinder, Cassius, your desires.°
I'll leave you.                                 35

CASSIUS.   Brutus, I do observe you now of late;
I have not° from your eyes that gentleness
And show of love as° I was wont to have.
You bear too stubborn and too strange a hand°
Over your friend that loves you.                40

BRUTUS.   Cassius,
Be not deceived. If I have veiled my look,
I turn the trouble of my countenance
Merely upon myself.° Vexèd I am

---

18 **press** crowd
20 **Caesar . . . hear** see I ii 225
21 **ides** midpoint, 15th day
26 **What . . . again** (Caesar evidently expects that the awe of his presence will either tongue-tie the man or alter his message)
28 s.d. **Sennet** trumpet flourish
28 s.d. **Mane[n]t** remain on stage (from Latin *maneo*)
29 **see . . . course** i.e. follow the race
32 **gamesome** (1) in a sportive mood (2) fond of games (with the implication that to be so is frivolous)

33 **quick** (1) speedy (in running) (2) lively (in mind)
34 **Let . . . desires** i.e. don't let my staying prevent your going
36-37 **I do . . . not** i.e. I notice of late that I have not
38 **as** that
39 **bear . . . hand** treat too harshly and coldly (literally, keep too tight a rein in managing a steed)
42-44 **If . . . myself** i.e. if I appear withdrawn, or cloudy, it is only to avoid troubling others with my problems

Of late with passions of some difference,°                    45
Conceptions only proper to° myself,
Which give some soil,° perhaps, to my behaviors;
But let not therefore my good friends be grieved
(Among which number, Cassius, be you one)
Nor construe any further° my neglect                          50
Than that poor Brutus, with himself at war,
Forgets the shows of love to other men.

CASSIUS.   Then, Brutus, I have much mistook your passion;°
By means whereof this breast of mine hath buried°
Thoughts of great value, worthy cogitations.                  55
Tell me, good Brutus, can you see your face?

BRUTUS.   No, Cassius;
For the eye sees not itself but by reflection,
By some other° things.

CASSIUS.   'Tis just.°                                        60
And it is very much lamented, Brutus,
That you have no such mirrors as will turn°
Your hidden worthiness into your eye,
That you might see your shadow.°
I have heard                                                  65
Where many of the best respect° in Rome
(Except immortal° Caesar), speaking of Brutus
And groaning underneath this age's yoke,
Have wished that noble Brutus had his eyes.°

BRUTUS.   Into what dangers would you                         70
Lead me, Cassius,
That you would have me seek into myself
For that which is not in me?°

CASSIUS.   Therefore,° good Brutus, be prepared to hear;
And since you know you cannot see yourself                    75

---

45  **of . . . difference** conflicting
46  **proper to** concerning
47  **soil** blemish
50  **construe . . . further** give any further
meaning to (*construe* was pronounced "cón-
ster")
53  **passion** feelings
54  **By . . . buried** i.e. because of this
"mistake," I have kept in my own breast
(instead of confiding to you)
59  **other** i.e. other than itself (e.g. a
mirror)
60  **just** true

62  **turn** turn back, i.e. reflect
64  **shadow** image
66  **respect** repute
67  **immortal** (spoken with irony)
69  **had his eyes** i.e. could see that
"yoke," together with the greatness in himself that might inspire his countrymen to
protest it
73  **that . . . me** i.e. the greatness you impute to me
74  **Therefore** on that point

So well as by reflection, I, your glass,°
Will modestly° discover to yourself
That of yourself which you yet know not of.
And be not jealous on° me, gentle Brutus.
Were I a common laughter,° or did use°                80
To stale° with ordinary oaths° my love
To every new protester;° if you know
That I do fawn on men and hug them hard,
And after scandal them;° or if you know
That I profess myself in banqueting°                85
To all the rout,° then hold me dangerous.

            *Flourish and shout.*

BRUTUS.   What means this shouting?
I do fear, the people choose Caesar
For their king.

CASSIUS.   Ay, do you fear it?                90
Then must I think you would not have it so.

BRUTUS.   I would not, Cassius; yet I love him well.
But wherefore do you hold me here so long?
What is it that you would impart to me?
If it be aught toward the general good,°                95
Set honor in one eye and death i' th' other,
And I will look on both indifferently;°
For let the gods so speed me as° I love
The name of honor more than I fear death.

CASSIUS.   I know that virtue to be in you, Brutus,                100
As well as I do know your outward favor.°
Well, honor is the subject of my story.
I cannot tell what you and other men
Think of this life; but for my single self,

---

76 **glass** mirror
77 **modestly** without exaggeration
79 **jealous on** suspicious of
80 **laughter** one who is laughed at, a trifler
80 **did use** accustomed
81 **stale** cheapen
81 **ordinary oaths** (1) hackneyed oaths (?) (2) tavern oaths (from ordinary-inn) (?)
82 **every . . . protester** i.e. every new acquaintance who protests (calls) himself my friend

84 **after . . . them** later slander them
85 **profess . . . banqueting** i.e. declare friendship for every one around me when drinking too much
86 **rout** rabble
95 **toward . . . good** that concerns the general welfare
97 **indifferently** impartially
98 **speed me as** favor me in proportion as
101 **favor** appearance

I had as lief not be° as live to be                              105
In awe of such a thing as I myself.°
I was born free as Caesar; so were you.
We both have fed as well, and we can both
Endure the winter's cold as well as he.
For once, upon a raw and gusty day,                             110
The troubled Tiber chafing with her shores,°
Caesar said to me, "Dar'st thou, Cassius, now
Leap in with me into this angry flood
And swim to yonder point?" Upon the word,
Accoutred° as I was, I plungèd in                               115
And bade him follow. So indeed he did.
The torrent roared, and we did buffet it
With lusty sinews, throwing it aside
And stemming° it with hearts of controversy.°
But ere we could arrive° the point proposed,                    120
Caesar cried, "Help me, Cassius, or I sink!"
I, as Aeneas,° our great ancestor,
Did from the flames of Troy upon his shoulder
The old Anchises bear, so from the waves of Tiber
Did I the tirèd Caesar. And this man                            125
Is now become a god, and Cassius is
A wretched creature and must bend his body°
If Caesar carelessly but nod on him.
He had a fever when he was in Spain,
And when the fit° was on him, I did mark°                       130
How he did shake. 'Tis true, this god did shake.
His coward lips did from their color fly,°
And that same eye whose bend° doth awe the world
Did lose his° luster. I did hear him groan.
Ay, and that tongue of his that bade the Romans                 135
Mark him and write his speeches in their books,

---

**105 had ... not be** would as soon not live
**106 such ... myself** i.e. a mere man (see
I i 75, I ii 67, 125-26, 131)
**111 chafing ... shores** i.e. stormy (dashing
her waves against her shores)
**115 Accoutred** dressed
**119 stemming** making headway against
**119 controversy** rivalry (with the torrent
and with each other)
**120 arrive** (here used in its root sense,
"to come to shore")
**122-24 Aeneas** legendary founder of Rome
and hero of Virgil's *Aeneid*. Aeneas escapes

from his native Troy (which the Greeks have
sacked and set afire) bearing his old father
Anchises on his back
**127 bend his body** bow
**130 fit** chill
**130 mark** observe
**132 did ... fly** turned pale (literally, they
behaved like cowardly soldiers deserting
their flag or "colors")
**133 bend** glance
**134 his** its

"Alas," it cried, "give me some drink, Titinius,"
As a sick girl! Ye gods, it doth amaze me
A man of such a feeble temper° should
So get the start of° the majestic° world                         140
And bear the palm° alone.

                    *Shout. Flourish.*

BRUTUS.    Another general shout?
I do believe that these applauses are
For some new honors that are heaped on Caesar.

CASSIUS.    Why, man, he doth bestride the narrow world          145
Like a Colossus,° and we petty men
Walk under his huge legs and peep about
To find ourselves dishonorable° graves.
Men at some time° are masters of their fates.
The fault, dear Brutus, is not in our stars,°                    150
But in ourselves, that we are underlings.
Brutus and Caesar: What should be in that "Caesar"?
Why should that name be sounded° more than yours?
Write them together: yours is as fair a name.
Sound them: it doth become the mouth as well.                    155
Weigh them: it is as heavy. Conjure with 'em:°
"Brutus" will start a spirit° as soon as "Caesar."
Now in the names of all the gods at once,
Upon what meat° doth this our Caesar feed
That he is grown so great? Age,° thou art shamed.               160
Rome, thou hast lost the breed° of noble bloods.
When went there by an age since the great Flood°
But it was famed with more than with° one man?

---

139  **temper** constitution
140  **get . . . of** get the jump on
140  **majestic** i.e. having a grandeur that makes Caesar's outstripping it all the more surprising
141  **palm** wreath of palms, the victor's prize
146  **Colossus** the giant statue of Apollo (one of the seven wonders of the ancient world), whose legs bestrid the harbor at Rhodes
148  **dishonorable** (because we have become Caesar's slaves)
149  **at . . . time** at a particular moment (see IV iii 244-45)
150  **stars** i.e. astrological destiny
153  **sounded** (1) pronounced (?) (2) celebrated (?)

156  **Conjure with 'em** (alluding to the belief that certain names and words had magical power to call up spirits)
157  **start a spirit** call up a ghost
159  **meat** food
160  **Age** i.e. the present age that "groans" under Caesar's "yoke" (see I ii 68)
161  **breed** (1) genealogical strain (?) (2) ability to produce (?)
162  **the . . . Flood** the dawn of time (when Zeus flooded the world and saved of all mortals only the virtuous Deucalion and his wife)
163  **famed . . . than with** famous for more than

When could they say (till now) that talked of Rome
That her wide walks° encompassed but one man?                165
Now is it Rome indeed, and room° enough,
When there is in it but one only man.
O, you and I have heard our fathers say
There was a Brutus° once that would have brooked°
Th' eternal devil° to keep his state° in Rome              170
As easily as a king.°

BRUTUS.   That you do love me I am nothing jealous.°
What you would work me to, I have some aim.°
How I have thought of this, and of these times,
I shall recount hereafter. For this present,°              175
I would not so (with love I might entreat you°)
Be any further moved.° What you have said
I will consider; what you have to say
I will with patience hear, and find a time
Both meet to° hear and answer such high° things.          180
Till then, my noble friend, chew° upon this:
Brutus had rather be a villager
Than to repute himself a son of Rome
.  Under these° hard conditions as this time
Is like to lay upon us.°                                    185

CASSIUS.   I am glad that my weak words
Have struck but thus much show of fire from Brutus.

                *Enter Caesar and his Train.*°

BRUTUS.   The games are done,
And Caesar is returning.

CASSIUS.   As they pass by,                                 190
Pluck Casca by the sleeve,

---

165  **walks**  public spaces
166  **Rome, room**  (in Elizabethan usage, both pronounced "room": "Rome" has "room enough" because it has only one true "man" in it: Caesar)
169  **Brutus**  Lucius Junius Brutus (from whom Marcus Brutus claimed descent), who liberated Rome from the tyranny of the Tarquins in 509 B.C. and founded the Roman Republic
169  **brooked**  endured
170  **Th' . . . devil**  i.e. the very devil (here pronounced "de'il") himself
170  **state**  court

171  **As . . . king**  i.e. as easily as he would have endured a king in Rome
172  **am . . . jealous**  do not doubt
173  **aim**  idea
175  **For this present**  at this time
176  **with . . . you**  i.e. if I may implore you as a friend
177  **moved**  urged
180  **Both meet to**  fit both to
180  **high**  i.e. as having reference to those in high place—specifically, Caesar
181  **chew**  meditate
184  **these**  such
184-85  **conditions . . . us**  see I ii 68
187 s.d.  **Train**  group of followers

And he will (after his sour fashion) tell you
What hath proceeded worthy note to-day.

BRUTUS.    I will do so. But look you, Cassius,
The angry spot doth glow on Caesar's brow,                    195
And all the rest look like a chidden train.
Calphurnia's cheek is pale, and Cicero
Looks with such ferret° and such fiery eyes
As we have seen him in the Capitol,
Being crossed in conference° by some senators.              200

CASSIUS.    Casca will tell us what the matter is.

CAESAR.    Antonius.

ANTONY.    Caesar?

CAESAR.    Let me have men about me that are fat,
Sleek-headed° men, and such as sleep a-nights.              205
Yond Cassius has a lean and hungry look.
He thinks too much. Such men are dangerous.

ANTONY.    Fear him not, Caesar; he's not dangerous.
He is a noble Roman, and well given.°

CAESAR.    Would he were fatter! But I fear him not.         210
Yet if my name were liable to fear,°
I do not know the man I should avoid
So soon as that spare Cassius. He reads much,
He is a great observer, and he looks
Quite through the deeds° of men. He loves no plays          215
As thou dost, Antony; he hears no music.°
Seldom he smiles, and smiles in such a sort°
As if he mocked himself and scorned his spirit
That° could be moved to smile at anything.
Such men as he be never at heart's ease                      220
Whiles they behold a greater than themselves,
And therefore are they very dangerous.

---

**198 ferret** ferret-like, i.e. small, intent,
red-eyed, and peevish
**200 crossed in conference** opposed in de-
bate
**205 sleek-headed** i.e. having hair that lies
smooth from careful grooming (a hint that
Cassius is disheveled and rumpled?)
**209 given** disposed
**211 if . . . to fear** if anyone with the
name Caesar could know fear

**215 Quite . . . deeds** i.e. to the motives
**216 he . . . music** (indifference to music,
the supreme art of "concord," is associated
here and elsewhere in Elizabethan literature with discord: cf. *Merchant of Venice,*
V i 83-88)
**217 sort** way
**218-19 his . . . That** i.e. the spirit of anyone who

I rather tell thee what is to be feared
Than what I fear; for always I am Caesar.°
Come on my right hand, for this ear is deaf,°                    225
And tell me truly what thou think'st of him.
     *Sennet. Exeunt Caesar and his Train. [Manet° Casca.]*

CASCA.   You pulled me by the cloak. Would you speak with
me?

BRUTUS.   Ay, Casca. Tell us what hath chanced to-day
That Caesar looks so sad.°

CASCA.   Why, you were with him, were you not?                 230

BRUTUS.   I should not then ask Casca what had chanced.

CASCA.   Why, there was a crown offered him; and being offered
him, he put it by° with the back of his hand—thus; and
then the people fell a-shouting.

BRUTUS.   What was the second noise for?                      235

CASCA.   Why, for that too.

CASSIUS.   They shouted thrice. What was the last cry for?

CASCA.   Why, for that too.

BRUTUS.   Was the crown offered him thrice?

CASCA.   Ay, marry,° was't! and he put it by thrice, every time     240
gentler than other;° and at every putting-by mine honest
neighbors shouted.

CASSIUS.   Who offered him the crown?

CASCA.   Why, Antony.

BRUTUS.   Tell us the manner of it, gentle Casca.               245

CASCA.   I can as well be hanged as tell the manner of it. It was
mere foolery; I did not mark° it. I saw Mark Antony offer
him a crown—yet 'twas not a crown neither, 'twas one of
these coronets°—and, as I told you, he put it by once; but
for all that, to my thinking, he would fain° have had it.     250

---

**224 Caesar** i.e. the name to which all fear
is foreign (note 211)
**225 Come . . . deaf** (Caesar's deafness is
brought to our attention just as he begins
to speak of himself as if he had no mortal
frailties)
**226 s.d. Manet** remains (see I ii 28 s.d.)
**229 sad** (1) serious (?) (2) sullen (?)
**233 put it by** refused it

**240 marry** indeed (in origin, a mild oath,
"by the Virgin Mary")
**241 than other** than the time before
**247 mark** notice (Casca pretends indifference, but in fact has noticed carefully, as
his story shows)
**249 coronets** i.e. small inferior crowns
**250 fain** gladly

Then he offered it to him again; then he put it by again;
but to my thinking, he was very loath to lay his fingers off
it. And then he offered it the third time. He put it the third
time by; and still° as he refused it, the rabblement hooted,°
and clapped their chopt° hands, and threw up their sweaty 255
nightcaps,° and uttered such a deal of stinking breath
because Caesar refused the crown that it had, almost,
choked Caesar; for he swounded° and fell down at it. And
for mine own part, I durst not laugh, for fear of opening
my lips and receiving the bad air. 260

CASSIUS. But soft,° I pray you. What, did Caesar swound?

CASCA. He fell down in the market place and foamed at mouth
and was speechless.

BRUTUS. 'Tis very like; he° hath the falling sickness.°

CASSIUS. No, Caesar hath it not; but you, and I, 265
And honest Casca, we have the falling sickness.°

CASCA. I know not° what you mean by that, but I am sure
Caesar fell down. If the tag-rag° people did not clap him
and hiss him, according as he pleased and displeased them,
as they use° to do the players in the theater, I am no true 270
man.

BRUTUS. What said he when he came unto himself?

CASCA. Marry, before he fell down, when he perceived the
common herd was glad he refused the crown, he plucked
me ope° his doublet and offered them his throat to cut. 275
An° I had been a man of any occupation,° if I would not
have taken him at a word° I would I might go to hell
among the rogues. And so he fell. When he came to himself again, he said, if he had done or said anything amiss,

---

254 **still** always
254 **hooted** cheered
255 **chopt** work-roughened (literally, chapped)
256 **nightcaps** hats (Casca speaks contemptuously)
258 **swounded** swooned
261 **soft** slowly
264 **like; he** probable, since it is well known that he
264 **falling sickness** epilepsy
266 **we have . . . sickness** i.e. our fortunes fall while Caesar's rise

267 **I know not** (Casca pretends not to understand the political implications of Cassius's remark)
268 **tag-rag** ragged (a tag is the torn piece of fabric that hangs from a tear)
270 **use** are accustomed
274-75 **plucked me ope** opened ("me" is frequently used after verbs in colloquial Elizabethan speech, not as object, but as a form of intensifier)
276 **An** if
276 **man . . . occupation** working man (i.e. one of the rabble looking on)
277 **at a word** immediately at his word

he desired their worships° to think it was° his infirmity. 280
Three or four wenches where I stood cried "Alas, good
soul!" and forgave him with all their hearts. But there's no
heed to be taken of them. If Caesar had stabbed their
mothers, they would have done no less.

BRUTUS.    And after that, he came thus sad° away?                285

CASCA.    Ay.

CASSIUS.    Did Cicero say anything?

CASCA.    Ay, he spoke Greek.

CASSIUS.    To what effect?

CASCA.    Nay, and° I tell you that, I'll ne'er look you i' th' face 290
again.° But those that understood him smiled at one
another and shook their heads; but for mine own part, it
was Greek to me.° I could tell you more news too. Marullus
and Flavius, for pulling scarfs° off Caesar's images, are put
to silence.° Fare you well. There was more foolery yet, if 295
I could remember it.

CASSIUS.    Will you sup with me to-night,° Casca?

CASCA.    No, I am promised forth.°

CASSIUS.    Will you dine with me to-morrow?

CASCA.    Ay, if I be alive, and your mind hold,° and your dinner 300
worth eating.

CASSIUS.    Good. I will expect you.

CASCA.    Do so. Farewell both.                                *Exit.*

BRUTUS.    What a blunt° fellow is this grown to be!
He was quick mettle° when he went to school.                        305

CASSIUS.    So is he now in execution
Of any bold or noble enterprise,
However° he puts on this tardy form.°

---

280 **their worships** Casca's sarcastic title
of respect for the rabble or, possibly, Caesar's own term to flatter them
280 **was** was owing to
285 **sad** (see 229)
290 **and** if
290-91..**ne'er . . . again** Casca affects
shame at the thought of knowing Greek
292-93 **it . . . me** i.e. I could make
nothing of it
294 **scarfs** see I i 65-66
294-95 **put to silence** suppressed

297 **Will . . . to-night** in this sudden in-
sistent invitation we are perhaps meant to
see Cassius's intent to gain another ad-
herent to the movement against Caesar
298 **promised forth** already committed
300 **hold** does not change
304 **blunt** dull-witted
305 **quick mettle** lively
308 **However** however much
308 **tardy form** slow-witted pose

This rudeness° is a sauce to his good wit,°
Which gives men stomach° to disgest° his words                310
With better appetite.

BRUTUS.    And so it is.
For this time° I will leave you.
To-morrow, if you please to speak with me,
I will come home to you; or if you will,                        315
Come home to me, and I will wait for you.

CASSIUS.    I will do so. Till then, think of the world.° *Exit Brutus.*
Well, Brutus, thou art noble; yet I see
Thy honorable mettle° may be wrought°
From that it is disposed.° Therefore it is meet              320
That noble minds keep ever with their likes;
For who so firm that cannot be seduced?
Caesar doth bear me hard;° but he loves Brutus.
If I were Brutus now and he were Cassius,
He should not humor° me. I will this night,                    325
In several hands,° in at his windows throw,
As if they came from several citizens,
Writings, all tending° to the great opinion
That Rome holds of his name; wherein obscurely
Caesar's ambition shall be glancèd° at.                         330
And after this let Caesar seat him sure,°
For we will shake him, or worse days endure.        *Exit.*

CICERO.    Good even, Casca. Brought° you Caesar home?
Why are you breathless? and why stare you so?

---

309  **rudeness**  i.e. simulated stupidity
309  **wit**  intelligence
310  **stomach**  appetite
310  **disgest**  digest
313  **For this time**  for the time being
317  **world**  current state of affairs
319  **mettle**  (1) spirit (2) metal
319  **wrought**  changed
320  **that . . . disposed**  its natural disposition

323  **bear me hard**  dislike me
324  **he**  i.e. Brutus
325  **humor**  move with flattery (i.e. as I am doing to *him*)
326  **hands**  handwritings
328  **tending**  pointing
330  **glancèd**  hinted
331  **him sure**  himself securely (in power)
I iii 1  **Brought**  escorted

CASCA.    Are you not moved when all the sway of earth°
Shakes like a thing unfirm?° O Cicero,
I have seen tempests when the scolding winds                    5
Have rived° the knotty oaks, and I have seen
Th' ambitious ocean swell and rage and foam
To be exalted with° the threat'ning clouds;
But never till to-night, never till now,
Did I go through a tempest dropping fire.                      10
Either there is a civil strife in heaven,
Or else the world, too saucy with the gods,
Incenses them to send destruction.

CICERO.    Why, saw you any thing more wonderful?°

CASCA.    A common slave (you know him well by sight)          15
Held up his left hand, which did flame and burn
Like twenty torches joined; and yet his hand,
Not sensible of° fire, remained unscorched.
Besides (I ha' not since put up my sword),
Against° the Capitol I met a lion,                            20
Who glazed° upon me, and went surly by
Without annoying me. And there were drawn
Upon a heap° a hundred ghastly° women,
Transformèd° with their fear, who swore they saw
Men, all in fire, walk up and down the streets.              25
And yesterday the bird of night° did sit
Even at noonday upon the market place,
Hooting and shrieking. When these prodigies
Do so conjointly meet,° let not men say
"These are their reasons—they are natural,"°                 30
For I believe they are portentous° things
Unto the climate° that they point upon.

CICERO.    Indeed it is a strange-disposèd time.
But men may construe things after their fashion,

---

3 **sway of earth** entire world
6 **rived** split
8 **exalted with** elevated to
14 **wonderful** remarkable (Cicero is inclined to take the storm as nothing special)
18 **sensible of** feeling
20 **Against** opposite
21 **glazed** glared
22-23 **drawn . . . heap** thronging together
23 **ghastly** ghostly, i.e. pale and spectral

24 **Transformèd** distraught, out of their wits
26 **bird of night** the owl, a bird of ill-omen
29 **conjointly meet** coincide
30 **"These . . . natural"** i.e. "Here are the explanations—therefore the events are no more than natural"
31 **portentous** i.e. offering a portent of things to come
32 **climate** region (in this case, Rome)

Clean from the purpose of the things themselves.°          35
Comes Caesar to the Capitol to-morrow?

CASCA.   He doth; for he did bid Antonius
Send word to you he would be there to-morrow.

CICERO.   Good night then, Casca.
This disturbèd sky is not to walk in.                      40

CASCA.   Farewell, Cicero.                          *Exit Cicero.*

*Enter Cassius.*

CASSIUS.   Who's there?

CASCA.   A Roman.

CASSIUS.   Casca, by your voice.

CASCA.   Your ear is good.                                 45
Cassius, what night is this!

CASSIUS.   A very pleasing night to honest° men.

CASCA.   Who ever knew the heavens menace so?

CASSIUS.   Those that have known the earth so full of faults.
For my part, I have walked about the streets,             50
Submitting me unto the perilous night,
And, thus unbracèd,° Casca, as you see,
Have bared my bosom to the thunder-stone;°
And when the cross° blue lightning seemed to open
The breast of heaven, I did present myself                55
Even in the aim and very flash of it.

CASCA.   But wherefore did you so much tempt the heavens?
It is the part of men to fear and tremble
When the most mighty gods by tokens° send
Such dreadful heralds to astonish° us.                    60

CASSIUS.   You are dull,° Casca:
And those sparks of life that should be in a Roman
You do want,° or else you use not.
You look pale, and gaze, and put on° fear,

---

**34-35  men . . . themselves** each may in-
terpret events in his own way, quite contrary to their real meaning
**47  honest** i.e. if a man is honorable, he
may take pleasure in knowing that the
heavens are not after *him* (see 50-56)
**52  unbracèd** with doublet open, i.e. in-
viting destruction

**53  thunder-stone** thunderbolt
**54  cross** forked
**59  tokens** signs (which Casca has described, 15 ff.)
**60  astonish** terrify
**61  dull** stupid (see I ii 304)
**63  want** lack
**64  put on** show

And cast yourself in° wonder,                                    65
To see the strange impatience° of the heavens;
But if you would consider the true cause—
Why all these fires, why all these gliding ghosts,
Why birds and beasts, from quality and kind;°
Why old° men, fools, and children calculate;°             70
Why all these things change from their ordinance,
Their natures, and preformèd faculties,
To monstrous quality°—why, you shall find
That heaven hath infused them with these spirits°
To make them instruments of fear and warning        75
Unto some monstrous state.°
Now could I, Casca, name to thee a man
Most like this dreadful night
That thunders, lightens, opens graves, and roars
As doth the lion in the Capitol;                                 80
A man no mightier than thyself or me
In personal action, yet prodigious° grown
And fearful,° as these strange eruptions are.

CASCA.   'Tis Caesar that you mean:
Is it not, Cassius?                                                    85

CASSIUS.   Let it be who it is. For Romans now
Have thews° and limbs like to their ancestors;
But woe the while!° our fathers' minds are dead,
And we are governed with our mothers' spirits;°
Our yoke and sufferance° show us womanish.          90

CASCA.   Indeed, they say the senators to-morrow
Mean to establish Caesar as a king,
And he shall wear his crown by sea and land
In every place save here in Italy.

---

65 **in** into
66 **impatience** turmoil
68-69 **Why all . . . kind** i.e. why everything seems to be behaving contrary to its
nature and species
70 **old** senile
70 **calculate** i.e. are suddenly gifted with
powers for calculating the future
71-73 **change . . . quality** i.e. change from
their established courses, their natures, and
the powers and limitations usually fixed in
them, to a character quite abnormal
74 **spirits** characteristics

76 **state** (1) state of affairs (see I ii 68,
160, 317) (2) political state (monstrous because Caesar would bring to the Roman
Republic the rule of one man)
82 **prodigious** portentous, ominous
83 **fearful** fear-causing
86-89 **Let . . . spirits** no matter whom I
mean, since Romans, though they may have
the physical attributes of their ancestors, no
longer have their indomitable spirit
87 **thews** sinews
88 **woe the while** woe be to the times
90 **sufferance** endurance (of the yoke)

CASSIUS.   I know where I will wear this dagger° then;          95
Cassius from bondage will deliver Cassius.
Therein,° ye gods, you make the weak most strong;
Therein, ye gods, you tyrants do defeat.°
Nor stony tower, nor walls of beaten brass,
Nor airless dungeon, nor strong links of iron,          100
Can be retentive to the strength of spirit;°
But life, being weary of these worldly bars,
Never lacks power to dismiss itself.
If I know this, know all the world besides,°
That part° of tyranny that I do bear          105
I can shake off at pleasure.                    *Thunder still.*

CASCA.   So can I.
So every bondman in his own hand bears
The power to cancel his captivity.

CASSIUS.   And why should Caesar be a tyrant then?          110
Poor man! I know he would not be a wolf
But that he sees the Romans are but sheep;
He were no lion, were not Romans hinds.°
Those that with haste will make a mighty fire
Begin it with weak straws. What trash is Rome,          115
What rubbish and what offal, when it serves
For the base matter to illuminate
So vile a thing as Caesar!° But, O grief,
Where  hast thou led me? I, perhaps, speak this
Before a willing bondman. Then I know          120
My answer must be made.° But I am armed,°
And dangers are to me indifferent.

CASCA.   You speak to Casca, and to such a man
That is no fleering° telltale. Hold,° my hand.
Be factious° for redress of all these griefs,          125

---

**95 where . . . dagger** i.e. plunged in my
heart
**97 Therein** i.e. in suicide
**98 you . . . defeat** i.e. you deprive tyrants of their victory
**99-101 Nor stony . . . spirit** i.e. they may
confine the body, but not the spirit
**104 know all . . . besides** let the rest of
the world take heed
**105 part** share
**113 hinds** (1) deer (2) cowardly servants
**114-18 Those . . . Caesar** as "weak straws"
serve to kindle even the mightiest blaze, so
*our* weaknesses ("trash," "rubbish," "offal")

feed the fire that makes Caesar bright (the
image seems to be that of a bonfire lighting up either a triumphal procession or a
statue)
**121 My . . . made** i.e. I shall be called to
account for what I have just said (since
Casca will inform on me)
**121 I am armed** (1) prepared in advance
for whatever fate may come (2) literally
armed so that I can deliver myself by
suicide
**124 fleering** hypocritically smiling
**124 Hold** stay a moment, look here
**125 Be factious** form a faction

And I will set this foot of mine as far
As who goes farthest.                    [*They shake hands.*]

CASSIUS.    There's a bargain made.
Now know you, Casca, I have moved already
Some certain of the noblest-minded Romans          130
To undergo with me an enterprise
Of honorable dangerous consequence;
And I do know, by this° they stay° for me
In Pompey's Porch;° for now, this fearful night,
There is no stir or walking in the streets,          135
And the complexion° of the element°
In favor's° like the work we have in hand,°
Most bloody, fiery, and most terrible.

*Enter Cinna.*

CASCA.    Stand close awhile, for here comes one in haste.

CASSIUS.    'Tis Cinna. I do know him by his gait.          140
He is a friend. Cinna, where haste you so?

CINNA.    To find out you. Who's that? Metellus Cimber?

CASSIUS.    No, it is Casca, one incorporate
To° our attempts. Am I not stayed for, Cinna?

CINNA.    I am glad on't.°          145
What a fearful night is this!
There's two or three of us have seen strange sights.

CASSIUS.    Am I not stayed for? Tell me.°

CINNA.    Yes, you are. O Cassius,
If you could but win the noble Brutus          150
To our party—

CASSIUS.    Be you content. Good Cinna, take this paper
And look you lay it in the praetor's chair,°

---

133 **this** this time
133 **stay** wait
134 **Pompey's Porch** portico of the theater built by Pompey the Great in 55 B.C., symbolically well-suited to be the conspirators' meeting place
136 **complexion** condition
136 **element** sky
137 **In favor's** in appearance is (the Folio reads "Is favors," which some editors amend to "Is fev'rous")
136-37 **And the . . . hand** i.e. the look of the sky is like the deed we must do
143-44 **incorporate To** intimately involved with (as if part of a single body or *corpus*)

145 **on't** of it (i.e. Casca's participation)
148 **Am . . . me** Cassius's insistence on hearing that he is "stayed for" may indicate that he, like Brutus, is not without vanity. If so, Cinna's immediate reference to the need for Brutus will be received, and Cassius's "Be you content" will be spoken, either with a certain coolness or perhaps with a touch of resignation. The play often places Cassius in the position of one who would like to lead and is equipped to do so, but who is not wholeheartedly followed, and knows it
153 **praetor's chair** Brutus's official chair as chief magistrate under the Consuls

Where Brutus may but° find it. And throw this
In at his window. Set this up with wax                          155
Upon old Brutus'° statue. All this done,
Repair° to Pompey's Porch, where you shall find us.
Is Decius° Brutus and Trebonius there?

CINNA.   All but Metellus Cimber, and he's gone
To seek you at your house. Well, I will hie°                     160
And so bestow these papers as you bade me.

CASSIUS.   That done, repair to Pompey's Theater.    *Exit Cinna.*
Come, Casca, you and I will yet ere° day
See Brutus at his house. Three parts of him
Is ours already, and the man entire                             165
Upon the next encounter yields him ours.

CASCA.   O, he sits high in all the people's hearts;
And that which would appear offense in us,
His countenance,° like richest alchemy,°
Will change to virtue and to worthiness.                        170

CASSIUS.   Him and his worth and our great need of him
You have right well conceited.° Let us go,
For it is after midnight; and ere day
We will awake him and be sure of him.          *Exeunt.*

*Enter Brutus in his orchard.*°                 II i

BRUTUS.   What,° Lucius, ho!
I cannot by the progress of the stars
Give guess how near to day. Lucius, I say!
I would it were my fault to sleep so soundly.
When,° Lucius, when? Awake, I say! What, Lucius!          5

---

**154  may but**  only may
**156  old Brutus'**  Lucius Junius Brutus (see
I ii 169)
**157  Repair**  go
**158  Decius Brutus**  actually Decimus Brutus,
a kinsman to the Brutus of the play
**160  hie**  hasten
**163  ere**  before
**169  countenance**  support

**169  alchemy**  the pseudoscience that sought
to convert base metal into gold—as Brutus's
participation will convert "offense" (168)
into "virtue" (170)
**172  conceited**  (1) conceived  (2) put into
a "conceit," (i.e. the alchemy comparison)
**II i s.d.  orchard**  garden
**1  What** ⎫  common exclamations of
**5  When** ⎭  impatience

*Enter Lucius.*

LUCIUS.    Called you, my lord?

BRUTUS.    Get me a taper° in my study, Lucius.
When it is lighted, come and call me here.

LUCIUS.    I will, my lord.                                          *Exit.*

BRUTUS.    It must be by his death; and for my part,            10
I know no personal cause to spurn at° him,
But for the general.° He would be crowned.
How that might change his nature, there's the question.
It is the bright day that brings forth the adder,
And that craves° wary walking. Crown him that,            15
And then I grant we put a sting in him°
That at his will he may do danger° with.
Th' abuse of greatness is,° when it disjoins
Remorse° from power. And to speak truth of Caesar,
I have not known when his affections swayed°            20
More than his reason. But 'tis a common proof°
That lowliness° is young ambition's ladder,
Whereto the climber upward turns his face;
But when he once attains the upmost round,°
He then unto the ladder turns his back,            25
Looks in the clouds, scorning the base degrees°
By which he did ascend. So Caesar may.
Then lest he may, prevent.° And since the quarrel
Will bear no color for the thing he is,
Fashion it thus:° that what he is, augmented,°            30

---

7 **taper** candle
11 **spurn at** attack
12 **But . . . general** except the general good
15 **craves** necessitates
15-16 **Crown . . . him** The sense is disputed. Some editors emend the text to: "Crown him? That?" or "Crown him—that!" where in both cases "that" refers to the action of crowning Caesar or, perhaps, to the condition of his being crowned. Others take the referent of "that" to be "king"; but as this word has nowhere been used in the preceding lines, it would be difficult if not impossible for an audience to understand it so. More plausible is to suppose that "that" refers to the condition of "bright day" (referred to in 14) which brings forth the adder. "If we confer on Caesar the quality of bright day," says Brutus, having somewhere in mind the traditional radiance of the regal crown, or even perhaps the normal Elizabethan association between sun and king,

"then of course we put a sting in him"— i.e. then we may reasonably expect the adder that bright day brings forth. By the "adder" and its "sting," Brutus appears to mean tyrannical rule. The soliloquy moves throughout not by logical progression, but by associative leaps, as here
17 **danger** harm
18 **is** i.e. arises
19 **Remorse** pity
20 **affections swayed** emotions ruled
21 **a . . . proof** a commonplace, i.e. something taken for granted
22 **lowliness** i.e. an appearance of humility
24 **round** rung
26 **base degrees** low steps
28 **prevent** forestall
28-30 **And since . . . thus** i.e. since what he is at present offers no pretext to support a bill of complaint ("the quarrel") against him, put the case as follows
30 **augmented** i.e. by kingly power

Would run to these and these extremities;°
And therefore think him as a serpent's egg,
Which, hatched, would as his kind° grow mischievous,
And kill him in the shell.

*Enter Lucius.*

LUCIUS.   The taper burneth in your closet,° sir.                          35
Searching the window° for a flint, I found
This paper, thus sealed up; and I am sure
It did not lie there when I went to bed.

*Gives him the letter.*

BRUTUS.   Get you to bed again; it is not day.
Is not to-morrow, boy, the ides of March?                                   40

LUCIUS.   I know not, sir.

BRUTUS.   Look in the calendar and bring me word.

LUCIUS.   I will, sir.                                           *Exit.*

BRUTUS.   The exhalations,° whizzing in the air,
Give so much light that I may read by them.                                 45

*Opens the letter and reads.*

"Brutus, thou sleep'st. Awake, and see thyself!
Shall Rome, &c.° Speak, strike, redress!"°

"Brutus, thou sleep'st. Awake!"
Such instigations have been often dropped
Where I have took them up.                                                  50
"Shall Rome, &c." ° Thus must I piece it out:
Shall Rome stand under one man's awe? What, Rome?
My ancestors did from the streets of Rome
The Tarquin drive when he was called a king.°
"Speak, strike, redress!" Am I entreated                                    55
To speak and strike? O Rome, I make thee promise,
If the redress will follow, thou receivest
Thy full petition at the hand of Brutus!°

*Enter Lucius.*

---

31 **extremities** extremes
33 **as his kind** as its nature is
35 **closet** study
36 **window** window area
44 **exhalations** meteors
47, 51 **&c.** (to be read out in full as *et cetera*. The phrase is part of the letter,

which is deliberately cryptic so that Brutus will have to "piece it out" (51) for himself)
47 **redress** put things right again
53-54 **My . . . king** I ii 169
57-58 **If . . . Brutus** i.e. if putting things right will be the result, Brutus will do all that Rome asks

LUCIUS.   Sir, March is wasted fifteen days.°        *Knock within.*

BRUTUS.   'Tis good. Go to the gate; somebody knocks.              60

                                           *[Exit Lucius.]*

    Since Cassius first did whet me against Caesar,
    I have not slept.
    Between the acting of a dreadful thing
    And the first motion,° all the interim is
    Like a phantasma° or a hideous dream.                          65
    The genius° and the mortal° instruments°
    Are then in council, and the state of a man,
    Like to a little kingdom, suffers then
    The nature of an° insurrection.°

                 *Enter Lucius.*

LUCIUS.   Sir, 'tis your brother° Cassius at the door,             70
    Who doth desire to see you.

BRUTUS.   Is he alone?

LUCIUS.   No, sir, there are moe° with him.

BRUTUS.   Do you know them?

LUCIUS.   No, sir. Their hats are plucked° about their ears       75
    And half their faces buried in their cloaks,
    That by no means I may discover° them
    By any mark of favor.°

BRUTUS.   Let 'em enter.                        *[Exit Lucius.]*
    They are the faction.° O conspiracy,                          80
    Sham'st thou° to show thy dang'rous brow by night,
    When evils are most free? O, then by day
    Where wilt thou find a cavern dark enough
    To mask thy monstrous visage? Seek none, conspiracy.
    Hide it in smiles and affability:                             85

---

**59   Sir . . . days** i.e. to-morrow is the ides
of March (see 40)
**64   motion** inner prompting to action
**65   phantasma** hallucination
**66   genius** attendant spirit thought to be
assigned to every individual at birth
**66   mortal** (1) causing death (when considered with reference to their murderous intent) (2) subject to death (when contrasted
with the attendant spirit, who is immortal)
**66   instruments** passions and other faculties of the human psyche
**69   The . . . an** a kind of

**67-69   the state . . . insurrection** i.e. insurrection in the state implies insurrection in
the individual who foments it—an Elizabethan commonplace
**70   brother** Cassius was married to Brutus's
sister
**73   moe** more
**75   plucked** pulled down
**77   discover** recognize
**78   favor** appearance
**80   faction** dissidents
**81   Sham'st thou** art thou ashamed (alluding to the concealments mentioned by
Lucius)

For if thou path,° thy native semblance on,°
Not Erebus° itself were dim enough
To hide thee from prevention.°

*Enter the Conspirators, Cassius, Casca, Decius, Cinna,*
*Metellus [Cimber], and Trebonius.*

CASSIUS.   I think we are too bold upon° your rest.
      Good morrow, Brutus. Do we trouble you?         90

BRUTUS.   I have been up this hour, awake all night.
      Know I these men that come along with you?

CASSIUS.   Yes, every man of them; and no man here
      But honors you; and every one doth wish
      You had but that opinion of yourself            95
      Which every noble Roman bears of you.
      This is Trebonius.

BRUTUS.   He is welcome hither.

CASSIUS.   This, Decius Brutus.

BRUTUS.   He is welcome too.                       100

CASSIUS.   This, Casca; this Cinna; and this, Metellus Cimber.

BRUTUS.   They are all welcome.
      What watchful cares° do interpose themselves
      Betwixt your eyes and night?

CASSIUS.   Shall I entreat a word?         *They° whisper.* 105

DECIUS.   Here lies the east. Doth not the day break here?°

CASCA.   No.

CINNA.   O, pardon, sir, it doth; and yon grey lines
      That fret° the clouds are messengers of day.

CASCA.   You shall confess that you are both deceived.     110
      Here, as I point my sword, the sun arises,

---

**86 path** walk about
**86 thy . . . on** i.e. wearing the "monstrous
visage" that is native to you
**87 Erebus** a gloomy region that souls
must pass through on their way to Hades
**88 prevention** being forestalled
**89 upon** in trespassing on
**103 watchful cares** worries that make you
watch, i.e. stay awake
**105 s.d. They** i.e. Brutus and Cassius
**106-16 Here . . . here** While Cassius confers with Brutus, the other conspirators en-
gage in inconsequential talk, as men often
do at moments of great tension. Even this
talk, however, is made to flood our minds
with images of their desperate errand: the
daybreak and sun rising recall the "bright
day" of Caesar (14) and his rising when he
is crowned king (21-27); Casca's sword
points symbolically in the direction from
which the sun will rise, and then in the direction of the Capitol, where in fact the
murder will take place; disagreement
among conspirators often foretells in Shakespeare disorder or disaster for their hopes;
etc.
**109 fret** cast a fretwork pattern on

Which is a great way growing° on the south,
Weighing° the youthful season of the year.
Some two months hence, up higher toward the north
He first presents his fire; and the high east                                    115
Stands as the Capitol, directly here.

BRUTUS.   Give me your hands all over, one by one.

CASSIUS.   And let us swear our resolution.

BRUTUS.   No, not an oath. If not the face of men,°
The sufferance° of our souls, the time's abuse°—                                120
If these be motives weak, break off betimes,°
And every man hence to his idle bed.
So let high-sighted° tyranny range on
Till each man drop by lottery.° But if these°
(As I am sure they do) bear fire enough                                          125
To kindle cowards and to steel with valor°
The melting spirits of women, then, countrymen,
What need we any spur but our own cause
To prick us to redress? what other bond
Than° secret Romans that have spoke the word°                                   130
And will not palter?° and what other oath
Than honesty to honesty engaged°
That this shall be,° or we will fall° for it?
Swear° priests and cowards and men cautelous,°
Old feeble carrions and such suffering souls                                     135
That welcome wrongs;° unto bad causes swear
Such creatures as men doubt;° but do not stain

---

112 **growing** encroaching
113 **Weighing** considering, i.e. because of
119 **the . . . men** i.e. the anxious or downcast looks of all true Romans, because they bear the yoke of these bad days
120 **sufferance** suffering
120 **the . . . abuse** the violation in these times of what ought to be (especially perhaps Caesar's overstepping the limits of authority proper for him in a Republic)
121 **betimes** quickly
123 **high-sighted** i.e. looking down from a great height like a falcon about to swoop on its prey (see I i 73-76)
124 **by lottery** at random (i.e. whenever the falcon swoops)
124 **these** these men
125-26 **bear . . . valor** In the composition of these lines, "fire" in its literal sense seems to have suggested "kindle," while in a more figurative sense it suggested "steel" —cf. "fire and steel," i.e. gun and sword. Therefore what Brutus is saying, not quite

logically, is that the conspirators have enough "fire" to kindle cowards and enough "steel" to stiffen women or womanish men
130 **Than** than the fact that we are
130 **the word** our word of honor
131 **palter** equivocate
132 **honesty . . . engaged** i.e. the pledge of one honest man to another
133 **this . . . be** i.e. we shall succeed in our purpose
133 **fall** die
134 **Swear** place on oath
134 **cautelous** overcautious
136 **That . . . wrongs** i.e. that must be put on oath to act because they are so spiritless that they do not resent, but welcome, injuries
136-37 **unto . . . doubt** i.e. if the cause you ask support for is bad, or if your colleagues are such as men mistrust ("doubt"), then you may have to resort to oath-swearing (but not for *this* cause and *these* men)

The even° virtue of our enterprise,
Nor th' insuppressive° mettle° of our spirits,
To think that or our cause or° our performance                    140
Did need an oath; when every drop of blood
That every Roman bears, and nobly bears,
Is guilty of a several° bastardy
If he do break the smallest particle
Of any promise that hath passed from him.                         145

CASSIUS.   But what of Cicero? Shall we sound him?°
I think he will stand very strong with us.

CASCA.   Let us not leave him out.

CINNA.   No, by no means.

METELLUS.   O, let us have him! for his silver hairs              150
Will purchase us a good opinion°
And buy men's voices° to commend our deeds.
It shall be said his judgment ruled our hands.
Our youths and wildness shall no whit° appear,
But all be buried in his gravity.°                                155

BRUTUS.   O, name him not! Let us not break° with him;
For he will never follow anything
That other men begin.°

CASSIUS.   Then leave him out.

CASCA.   Indeed he is not fit.                                    160

DECIUS.   Shall no man else be touched but only Caesar?

CASSIUS.   Decius, well urged. I think it is not meet°
Mark Antony, so well beloved of Caesar,
Should outlive Caesar. We shall find of° him
A shrewd° contriver; and you know, his means,°                    165

---

**138  even**  steadfast
**139  insuppressive**  insuppressible
**139  mettle**  see note I i 62
**140  or . . . or**  either . . . or
**143  several**  separate
**146  sound him**  sound him out
**151  opinion**  reputation
**152  voices**  (used partly in the sense of "votes")
**154  no whit**  not at all
**155  gravity**  i.e. grave authority as an older statesman
**150-55  O, let . . . gravity**  that Casca wishes for the "alchemy" of Brutus to turn "offense" to "virtue" (I iii 167-70), and Metel-

lus for Cicero's "gravity" to bury their "youths and wildness," is Shakespeare's indication to us of the doubts that beset the conspirators' cause, even in their own minds
**156  break**  take the matter up
**157-58  For . . . begin**  this objection may mean that Brutus wishes no rival in the undertaking against Caesar; his fellow conspirators' response to it shows how complete his influence over them is (see 350-51)
**162  meet**  suitable
**164  of**  in
**165  shrewd**  troublesome
**165  his means**  i.e. the resources at his disposal

If he improve° them, may well stretch so far
As to annoy° us all; which to prevent,°
Let Antony and Caesar fall together.

BRUTUS.   Our course will seem too bloody, Caius Cassius,
To cut the head off and then hack the limbs,                      170
Like wrath in death and envy afterwards;°
For Antony is but a limb of Caesar.
Let's be sacrificers, but not butchers, Caius.
We all stand up against the spirit of Caesar,
And in the spirit of men there is no blood.                       175
O that we then could come by° Caesar's spirit
And not dismember Caesar! But, alas,
Caesar must bleed for it! And, gentle friends,
Let's kill him boldly, but not wrathfully;
Let's carve him as a dish fit for the gods,                       180
Not hew him as a carcass fit for hounds.
And let our hearts, as subtle masters do,
Stir up their servants° to act of rage
And after seem to chide 'em. This shall make
Our purpose necessary, and not envious;                           185
Which so appearing to the common eyes,
We shall be called purgers,° not murderers.
And for Mark Antony, think not of him;
For he can do no more than Caesar's arm
When Caesar's head is off.                                        190

CASSIUS.   Yet I fear him;
For in the ingrafted° love he bears to Caesar—

BRUTUS.   Alas, good Cassius, do not think of him!
If he love Caesar, all that he can do
Is to himself—take thought, and die° for Caesar.                 195
And that were much he should;° for he is given
To sports, to wildness, and much company.

---

166  **improve**  use
167  **annoy**  injure
167  **prevent**  forestall
171  **Like . . . afterwards**  i.e. as if all had
been done in spiteful passion—the assassination of Caesar in "wrath" and the assassination of Antony (or others) in "envy"—
instead of, as Brutus likes to think, ration-
ally and sacrificially
176  **by**  at

183  **their servants**  (1) the feelings (?)  (2)
the hands (?)
187  **purgers**  healers
192  **ingrafted**  deeply implanted
195  **take . . . die**  brood despondently and
pine away
196  **that were . . . should**  that would be
too much to expect of him

TREBONIUS.    There is no fear° in him. Let him not die;
> For he will live, and laugh at this hereafter.    *Clock strikes*.

BRUTUS.    Peace! Count the clock.                                    200

CASSIUS.    The clock hath stricken three.

TREBONIUS.    'Tis time to part.

CASSIUS.    But it is doubtful yet
> Whether° Caesar will come forth to-day or no;
> For he is superstitious grown of late,                              205
> Quite from° the main° opinion he held once
> Of fantasy,° of dreams, and ceremonies.°
> It may be these apparent° prodigies,
> The unaccustomed terror of this night,
> And the persuasion of his augurers°                                 210
> May hold him from the Capitol to-day.

DECIUS.    Never fear that. If he be so resolved,
> I can o'ersway° him; for he loves to hear
> That unicorns may be betrayed with trees°
> And bears with glasses,° elephants with holes,°                     215
> Lions with toils,° and men with flatterers;
> But when I tell him he hates flatterers,
> He says he does, being then most flatterèd.
> Let me work;
> For I can give his humor° the true bent°                            220
> And I will bring him to the Capitol.

CASSIUS.    Nay, we will all of us be there to fetch him.

BRUTUS.    By the eighth° hour. Is that the uttermost?°

CINNA.    Be that the uttermost, and fail not then.

---

198  **no fear**  nothing to fear
204  **Whether**  (pronounced as one syllable: "whe'r")
206  **from**  different from
206  **main**  strong (cf. "with might and main")
207  **fantasy**  fancy, i.e. imaginary terrors
207  **ceremonies**  omens (see II ii 14)
208  **apparent**  obvious
210  **augurers**  i.e. augurs, priests whose function was to predict future events
213  **o'ersway**  persuade
214  **with trees**  i.e. by the hunter's dodging behind a tree so that the charging animal drove his horn into the trunk and thus was caught

215  **glasses**  mirrors to dazzle or distract them
215  **holes**  concealed pits
216  **toils**  nets
220  **humor**  disposition
220  **true bent**  right inclination
223  **eighth**  (the wording of the Fourth Folio; the First Folio has "eight")
223  **uttermost**  latest

METELLUS.    Caius Ligarius doth bear Caesar hard,°        225
Who rated° him for speaking well of Pompey.
I wonder none of you have thought of him.

BRUTUS.    Now, good Metellus, go along by him.°
He loves me well, and I have given him reasons.°
Send him but hither, and I'll fashion° him.        230

CASSIUS.    The morning comes upon 's.
We'll leave you, Brutus.
And, friends, disperse yourselves; but all remember
What you have said and show yourselves true Romans.

BRUTUS.    Good gentlemen, look fresh and merrily.        235
Let not our looks put on° our purposes,
But bear it° as our Roman actors do,
With untired spirits and formal constancy.°
And so good morrow to you every one.
                                    *Exeunt. Manet Brutus.*
Boy! Lucius! Fast asleep? It is no matter.        240
Enjoy the honey-heavy dew of slumber.
Thou hast no figures nor no fantasies°
Which busy care draws in the brains of men;
Therefore thou sleep'st so sound.

                        *Enter Portia.*

PORTIA.    Brutus, my lord.        245

BRUTUS.    Portia! What mean you? Wherefore rise you now?
It is not for your health thus to commit
Your weak condition to the raw cold morning.

PORTIA.    Nor for yours neither. Y' have ungently, Brutus,
Stole from my bed. And yesternight at supper        250
You suddenly arose and walked about,
Musing and sighing with your arms across;°
And when I asked you what the matter was,
You stared upon me with ungentle looks.
I urged you further; then you scratched your head        255
And too impatiently stamped with your foot.

---

225  **bear Caesar hard**  see note I ii 323
226  **rated**  berated
228  **him**  i.e. his house
229  **reasons**  i.e. reasons for his affection, by favors I have done him
230  **fashion**  shape (to our ends)
236  **put on**  show

237  **bear it**  act
238  **formal constancy**  dignified self-possession
242  **figures, fantasies**  imaginations (of things that must be done)
252  **across**  folded (a supposed sign of melancholy)

Yet I insisted; yet you answered not,
But with an angry wafter° of your hand
Gave sign for me to leave you. So I did,
Fearing to strengthen that impatience                                    260
Which seemed too much enkindled, and withal°
Hoping it was but an effect of humor,°
Which sometime hath his° hour with every man.
It will not let you eat nor talk nor sleep,
And could it work so much upon your shape                                 265
As it hath much prevailed on your condition,°
I should not know you Brutus. Dear my lord,
Make me acquainted with your cause of grief.

BRUTUS.   I am not well in health, and that is all.

PORTIA.   Brutus is wise and, were he not in health,                      270
He would embrace the means to come by it.°

BRUTUS.   Why, so I do. Good Portia, go to bed.

PORTIA.   Is Brutus sick, and is it physical°
To walk unbracèd° and suck up the humors°
Of the dank morning? What, is Brutus sick,                                275
And will he steal out of his wholesome bed
To dare the vile contagion of the night,°
And tempt° the rheumy° and unpurgèd air,
To add unto his sickness? No, my Brutus.
You have some sick offense° within your mind,                             280
Which by the right and virtue of my place°
I ought to know of; and upon my knees
I charm° you, by my once commended beauty,
By all your vows of love, and that great vow
Which did incorporate° and make us one,                                   285
That you unfold to me, your self, your half,
Why you are heavy°—and what men to-night
Have had resort to you; for here have been

---

258 **wafter** waving
261 **withal** yet
262 **an . . . humor** a passing mood
263 **his** its
266 **condition** disposition
270-71 **Brutus . . . it** i.e. he would not be
up half the night, as now
273 **physical** curative
274 **unbracèd** see I iii 52
274 **humors** moistures

277 **night** i.e. the night air (which was
considered harmful)
278 **tempt** risk
278 **rheumy** (1) moist (2) rheum-produc-
ing (rheum is the discharge from the eyes,
nose, and mouth caused by taking cold)
280 **sick offense** offending ailment
281 **place** i.e. as your wife
283 **charm** conjure
285 **incorporate** make us one flesh
287 **heavy** sad

Some six or seven, who did hide their faces
Even from darkness.                                           290

BRUTUS.    Kneel not, gentle Portia.

PORTIA.    I should not need if you were gentle Brutus.°
Within the bond of marriage, tell me, Brutus,
Is it excepted° I should know no secrets
That appertain to you? Am I your self                        295
But, as it were, in sort or limitation?°
To keep with you at meals, comfort your bed,
And talk to you sometimes? Dwell I but in the suburbs°
Of your good pleasure? If it be no more,
Portia is Brutus' harlot, not his wife.                      300

BRUTUS.    You are my true and honorable wife,
As dear to me as are the ruddy drops°
That visit my sad heart.

PORTIA.    If this were true, then should I know this secret.
I grant I am a woman; but withal°                            305
A woman that Lord Brutus took to wife.
I grant I am a woman; but withal
A woman well-reputed, Cato's° daughter.
Think you I am no stronger than my sex,
Being so fathered and so husbanded?                          310
Tell me your counsels;° I will not disclose 'em.
I have made strong proof of my constancy,°
Giving myself a voluntary wound
Here, in the thigh. Can I bear that with patience,
And not my husband's secrets?                                315

BRUTUS.    O ye gods,
Render me worthy of this noble wife!            *Knock.*
Hark, hark! One knocks. Portia, go in awhile,
And by and by thy bosom shall partake
The secrets of my heart.                                     320

---

**292 gentle Brutus** alluding to his calling
her "gentle Portia"
**294 excepted** singled out as an exception
that
**296 in sort or limitation** in a way or
within certain limits (these are legal terms
like "exception" in 294)
**298 suburbs** i.e. (1) areas removed from
the center (of his "good pleasure") (2)

areas favored (in Elizabethan London) for
brothels (cf. "harlot" in 300)
**302 ruddy drops** (of blood)
**305 withal** nevertheless
**308 Cato** Cato Uticensis, a strong supporter of Pompey, who had killed himself in 46
B.C.
**311 counsels** secrets
**312 constancy** resoluteness

All my engagements° I will construe° to thee,
All the charactery of my sad brows.°
Leave me with haste.                    *Exit Portia.*
Lucius, who's that knocks?

*Enter Lucius and [Caius] Ligarius.*

LUCIUS.  Here is a sick man that would speak with you.    325

BRUTUS.  Caius Ligarius, that Metellus spake of.
Boy, stand aside. Caius Ligarius, how?°

CAIUS.  Vouchsafe° good morrow from a feeble tongue.

BRUTUS.  O, what a time have you chose out, brave Caius,
To wear a kerchief!° Would you were not sick!    330

CAIUS.  I am not sick if Brutus have in hand
Any exploit worthy the name of honor.

BRUTUS.  Such an exploit have I in hand, Ligarius,
Had you a healthful ear to hear of it.

CAIUS.  By all the gods that Romans bow before,    335
I here discard my sickness! [*Throws off his kerchief.*] Soul
of Rome,
Brave son derived from honorable loins,°
Thou like an exorcist° has conjured up
My mortifièd° spirit. Now bid me run,
And I will strive with things impossible;    340
Yea, get the better of them. What's to do?

BRUTUS.  A piece of work
That will make sick men whole.°

CAIUS.  But are not some whole that we must make sick?

BRUTUS.  That must we also. What it is, my Caius,    345
I shall unfold to thee as we are going
To whom° it must be done.

---

321 **engagements** commitments
321 **construe** explain
322 **charactery . . . brows** what is written on my anxious face (*charactery* is pronounced charáctery)
327 **how** how goes it
328 **Vouchsafe** be good enough to accept
330 **kerchief** (worn when one was ill as protection against draughts)

337 **derived . . . loins** see note I ii 169
338 **exorcist** one who has power over spirits
339 **mortifièd** dying
343 **whole** i.e. hale, well
347 **To whom** to the house of him to whom

CAIUS.   Set on° your foot,
    And with a heart new-fired I follow you,
    To do I know not what; but it sufficeth                    350
    That Brutus leads me on.                    *Thunder.*
BRUTUS.   Follow me then.                    *Exeunt.*

*Thunder and lightning. Enter Julius Caesar, in his nightgown.*°    II ii
CAESAR.   Nor heaven nor earth
    Have been at peace to-night.
    Thrice hath Calphurnia in her sleep cried out
    "Help, ho! They murder Caesar!" Who's within?°
             *Enter a Servant.*
SERVANT.   My lord?                    5
CAESAR.   Go bid the priests do present° sacrifice,
    And bring me their opinions of success.°
SERVANT.   I will, my lord.                    *Exit.*
            *Enter Calphurnia.*
CALPHURNIA.   What mean you, Caesar? Think you to walk
    forth?
    You shall not stir out of your house to-day.                    10
CAESAR.   Caesar shall forth. The things that threatened me
    Ne'er looked but on my back. When they shall see
    The face of Caesar, they are vanishèd.°
CALPHURNIA.   Caesar, I never stood on ceremonies,°
    Yet now they fright me. There is one within,                    15
    Besides the things that we have heard and seen,
    Recounts° most horrid sights seen by the watch.°

---

**348 Set on** advance
**II ii s.d.  nightgown** dressing gown
**4 Who's within** i.e. he calls for a servant
**6 present** immediate
**7 success** the result (i.e. whether the omens are good or evil)

**11-13 Caesar . . . vanishèd** Caesar puts on his "public" self here, as he usually does when there is any threat to his pose of imperturbability (see I ii 20 ff, 211 ff, 223 ff; below, 47 ff, and III i, esp. 63 ff)
**14 stood on ceremonies** heeded omens
**17 Recounts** i.e. who recounts
**17 watch** night watchmen

A lioness hath whelpèd in the streets,
And graves have yawned and yielded up their dead.
Fierce fiery warriors fought upon the clouds　　　　　　　20
In ranks and squadrons and right form of war,°
Which drizzled blood upon the Capitol.
The noise of battle hurtled° in the air,
Horses did neigh, and dying men did groan,
And ghosts did shriek and squeal about the streets.　　25
O Caesar, these things are beyond all use,°
And I do fear them!

CAESAR.　What can be avoided
Whose end is purposed by the mighty gods?
Yet° Caesar shall go forth; for these predictions　　30
Are to the world in general as° to Caesar.

CALPHURNIA.　When beggars die there are no comets seen;
The heavens themselves blaze forth° the death of princes.

CAESAR.　Cowards die many times before their deaths;
The valiant never taste of death but once.　　　　　　35
Of all the wonders that I yet have heard,
It seems to me most strange that men should fear,
Seeing that death, a necessary end,
Will come when it will come.

*Enter a Servant.*

What say the augurers?　　　　　　　　　　　40

SERVANT.　They would not have you to stir forth to-day.
Plucking the entrails of an offering forth,
They could not find a heart within the beast.

CAESAR.　The gods do this in shame of cowardice.
Caesar should be a beast without a heart　　　　　　45
If he should stay at home to-day for fear.
No, Caesar shall not. Danger knows full well
That Caesar is more dangerous than he.
We are two lions littered in one day,
And I the elder and more terrible,　　　　　　　　50
And Caesar shall go forth.

---

**21 right . . . war** i.e. all the usual military formations
**23 hurtled** clattered
**26 use** customary experience
**30 Yet** i.e. in spite of all

**31 Are to . . . as** pertain to . . . as much as
**33 blaze forth** (1) show forth in fire (as last night) (2) proclaim—as if a herald with trumpet (as for all public announcements). "Blaze" = blow a musical instrument

CALPHURNIA.   Alas, my lord,
Your wisdom is consumed in confidence.°
Do not go forth to-day. Call it my fear
That keeps you in the house and not your own.                    55
We'll send Mark Antony to the Senate House,
And he shall say you are not well to-day.
Let me upon my knee prevail in this.

CAESAR.   Mark Antony shall say I am not well,
And for thy humor° I will stay at home.                          60

*Enter Decius.*

Here's Decius Brutus; he shall tell them so.

DECIUS.   Caesar, all hail! Good morrow, worthy Caesar;
I come to fetch you to the Senate House.

CAESAR.   And you are come in very happy° time
To bear my greeting to the senators                              65
And tell them that I will not come to-day.
Cannot, is false; and that I dare not, falser:
I will not come to-day. Tell them so, Decius.

CALPHURNIA.   Say he is sick.

CAESAR.   Shall Caesar send a lie?°                              70
Have I in conquest stretched mine arm so far
To be afeard to tell greybeards the truth?
Decius, go tell them Caesar will not come.

DECIUS.   Most mighty Caesar, let me know some cause,
Lest I be laughed at when I tell them so.                        75

CAESAR.   The cause is in my will: I will not come.
That is enough to satisfy the Senate;
But for your private satisfaction,
Because I love you, I will let you know.
Calphurnia here, my wife, stays° me at home.                     80
She dreamt to-night° she saw my statue,°
Which, like a fountain with an hundred spouts,
Did run pure blood; and many lusty Romans
Came smiling and did bathe their hands in it.

---

53  **confidence**  i.e. overconfidence
60  **humor**  whim
64  **happy**  opportune
70  **Shall . . . lie**  (a notable example of
Caesar's "public" pose; contrast it with 59,
where the same lie is approved)

80  **stays**  detains
81  **to-night**  i.e. last night
81  **statue**  (three syllables)

And these does she apply for° warnings and portents                    85
And evils imminent, and on her knee
Hath begged that I will stay at home to-day.

DECIUS.  This dream is all amiss interpreted;
It was a vision fair and fortunate.
Your statue spouting blood in many pipes,                              90
In which so many smiling Romans bathed,
Signifies that from you great Rome shall suck
Reviving blood, and that great men shall press
For° tinctures, stains, relics, and cognizance.°
This by Calphurnia's dream is signified.                               95

CAESAR.  And this way have you well expounded it.

DECIUS.  I have, when you have heard what I can say;
And know it now. The Senate have concluded
To give this day a crown to mighty Caesar.
If you shall send them word you will not come,                        100
Their minds may change. Besides, it were a mock
Apt to be rendered,° for some to say
"Break up the Senate till another time,
When Caesar's wife shall meet with better dreams."
If Caesar hide himself, shall they not whisper                        105
"Lo, Caesar is afraid"?
Pardon me, Caesar; for my dear dear love
To your proceeding° bids me tell you this,
And reason to my love is liable.°

CAESAR.  How foolish do your fears seem now, Calphurnia!             110
I am ashamèd I did yield to them.
Give me my robe, for I will go.

          *Enter Brutus, Ligarius, Metellus, Casca,*
               *Trebonius, Cinna, and Publius.*

And look where Publius is come to fetch me.

PUBLIUS.  Good morrow, Caesar.

---

**85 for** as
**93-94 press For** press forward to obtain
**94 tinctures . . . cognizance** i.e. some
visible show or sign of your life-giving
power. (In "tinctures," "stains," and "cognizance," Decius refers to the colorings and
markings in armorial coats and liveries such
as the followers of a king might seek from
him; in "relics," he refers to the wonder-
working remains of saints and martyrs. Are
we meant to infer that under the quick wit

of Decius's reinterpretation of Caesar's
dream that a republican distaste for "following" and wearing livery mixes uneasily
with a prophetic sense that the slain Caesar
will actually be regarded as a martyr?)
**101-2 mock . . . rendered** sarcasm likely
to be uttered
**108 proceeding** (1) advancement (?) (2) all
that concerns you (?)
**109 liable** subordinate

CAESAR.    Welcome, Publius.                                        115
    What, Brutus, are you stirred so early too?
    Good morning, Casca. Caius Ligarius,
    Caesar was ne'er so much your enemy°
    As that same ague which hath made you lean.
    What is't o'clock?                                             120

BRUTUS.    Caesar, 'tis strucken eight.°

CAESAR.    I thank you for your pains and courtesy.

                *Enter Antony.*

    See! Antony, that revels long a-nights,
    Is notwithstanding up. Good morrow, Antony.

ANTONY.    So° to most noble Caesar.                               125

CAESAR.    Bid them prepare° within.
    I am to blame to be thus waited for.
    Now, Cinna. Now, Metellus. What, Trebonius;°
    I have an hour's talk in store for you;
    Remember that you call on me to-day;                           130
    Be near me, that I may remember you.

TREBONIUS.    Caesar, I will. [*aside*] And so near will I be
    That your best friends shall wish I had been further.

CAESAR.    Good friends, go in and taste some wine with me,
    And we (like friends) will straightway go together.           135

BRUTUS.    [*aside*] That every like is not the same,° O Caesar,
    The heart of Brutus erns° to think upon.        *Exeunt.*

                *Enter Artemidorus, [reading a paper].*          *II iii*

[ARTEMIDORUS.]    "Caesar, beware of Brutus; take heed of
    Cassius; come not near Casca; have an eye to Cinna; trust

---

118  **enemy** Ligarius, like Cassius, Brutus,
and Cicero, had been a supporter of
Pompey
121  **Caesar . . . eight** this stress on the
clock's striking seems calculated to remind
us of that other clock whose ominous strike
we heard from Brutus's orchard (II i 200)
125  **So** i.e. the same wish
126  **prepare** i.e. set out wine (see 134)

128  **Now, Cinna . . . Trebonius** Caesar evidently shakes their hands in greeting
136  **every . . . same** things which look
alike are not in fact alike (i.e. not all your
apparent friends are in fact your friends)
137  **erns** yearns, grieves (we are never allowed to forget that Brutus and Caesar have
been close friends)

not Trebonius; mark well Metellus Cimber; Decius Brutus
loves thee not; thou has wronged Caius Ligarius. There is
but one mind in all these men, and it is bent° against  5
Caesar. If thou beest not immortal, look about you. Security
gives way to conspiracy.° The mighty gods defend thee!
                                        "Thy lover,°
                                        "ARTEMIDORUS."

Here will I stand till Caesar pass along                         10
And as a suitor° will I give him this.
My heart laments that virtue cannot live
Out of the teeth of emulation.°
If thou read this, O Caesar, thou mayest live;
If not, the Fates with traitors do contrive.°          *Exit.* 15

                    *Enter Portia and Lucius.*                    II iv

PORTIA.    I prithee, boy, run to the Senate House.
           Stay not to answer me, but get thee gone!
           Why dost thou stay?

LUCIUS.    To know my errand, madam.

PORTIA.    I would have had thee there and here again       5
           Ere I can tell thee what thou shouldst do there.
           [*Aside*] O constancy,° be strong upon my side,
           Set a huge mountain 'tween my heart and tongue!
           I have a man's mind, but a woman's might.°
           How hard it is for women to keep counsel!°        10
           Art thou here yet?

LUCIUS.    Madam, what should I do?
           Run to the Capitol and nothing else?
           And so return to you and nothing else?

---

II iii 5  **bent**  (like a bow)
6-7  **Security . . . conspiracy**  your lack of
caution about your safety opens the way to
conspiracy
8  **lover**  devoted friend
11  **as a suitor**  as if a petitioner
13  **out . . . emulation**  away from the
wounds that envious rivalry inflicts on it

15  **contrive**  conspire
II iv 7  **constancy**  resolution
9  **might**  strength
10  **keep counsel**  keep a secret (we are to
assume that Portia has been told of Brutus's
intents)

PORTIA.    Yes, bring me word, boy, if thy lord look well,                    15
For he went sickly forth; and take good note
What Caesar doth, what suitors press to him.
Hark, boy! What noise is that?

LUCIUS.    I hear none, madam.

PORTIA.    Prithee listen well.                                               20
I heard a bustling rumor° like a fray,°
And the wind brings it from the Capitol.

LUCIUS.    Sooth,° madam, I hear nothing.

*Enter the Soothsayer.*

PORTIA.    Come hither, fellow. Which way hast thou been?

SOOTHSAYER.    At mine own house, good lady.                                  25

PORTIA.    What is't o'clock?°

SOOTHSAYER.    About the ninth hour, lady.

PORTIA.    Is Caesar yet gone to the Capitol?

SOOTHSAYER.    Madam, not yet. I go to take my stand,
To see him pass on to the Capitol.                                           30

PORTIA.    That hast some suit° to Caesar, hast thou not?

SOOTHSAYER.    That I have, lady, if it will please Caesar
To be so good to Caesar as to hear me:
I shall beseech him to befriend himself.

PORTIA.    Why, know'st thou any harm's intended towards him?    35

SOOTHSAYER.    None that I know will be, much that I fear may
chance.°
Good morrow to you. Here the street is narrow.
The throng that follows Caesar at the heels,
Of senators, of praetors, common suitors,
Will crowd a feeble man almost to death.                                     40
I'll get me to a place more void° and there
Speak to great Caesar as he comes along.                    *Exit.*

PORTIA.    I must go in.
Ay me, how weak a thing
The heart of woman is! O Brutus,                                             45

---

21  **rumor** noise
21  **fray** battle
23  **Sooth** truly
26  **What is't o'clock** mention of the clock
again quickens the suspense

31  **suit** petition
36  **chance** happen
41  **void** empty

The heavens speed° thee in thine enterprise!
Sure the boy heard me.—Brutus hath a suit
That Caesar will not grant.°—O, I grow faint.—
Run, Lucius, and commend me° to my lord;
Say I am merry.° Come to me again                    50
And bring me word what he doth say to thee.

        *Exeunt [severally].*

*Flourish. Enter Caesar, Brutus, Cassius, Casca, Decius,* III i
*Metellus, Trebonius, Cinna, Antony, Lepidus, Artemidorus,*
  *[Popilius,] Publius, and the Soothsayer.*

CAESAR. The ides of March are come.

SOOTHSAYER. Ay, Caesar, but not gone.

ARTEMIDORUS. Hail, Caesar! Read this schedule.°

DECIUS. Trebonius doth desire you to o'erread
(At your best leisure) this his humble suit.°                    5

ARTEMIDORUS. O Caesar, read mine first; for mine's a suit
That touches° Caesar nearer. Read it, great Caesar!

CAESAR. What touches us ourself shall be last served.

ARTEMIDORUS. Delay not, Caesar! Read it instantly!

CAESAR. What, is the fellow mad?                    10

PUBLIUS. Sirrah,° give place.°

CASSIUS. What, urge you your petitions in the street?
Come to the Capitol.

  *[Caesar goes to the Capitol, the rest following.]*

POPILIUS. I wish your enterprise to-day may thrive.

CASSIUS. What enterprise, Popilius?                    15

POPILIUS. Fare you well.   *[Advances to Caesar.]*

---

**46 speed** favor
**47-48 Brutus . . . grant** (spoken to Lucius
to make her wish (46) sound harmless)
**49 commend me** give my love
**50 merry** in good spirits
**III i 3 schedule** scroll

**5 suit** request
**7 touches** concerns
**11 Sirrah** (patronizing form of address to
one of subordinate rank)
**11 give place** make way

BRUTUS.   What said Popilius Lena?

CASSIUS.   He wished to-day our enterprise might thrive.
I fear our purpose is discoverèd.

BRUTUS.   Look how he makes° to Caesar. Mark him.                    20

CASSIUS.   Casca,° be sudden,° for we fear prevention.°
Brutus, what shall be done? If this be known,
Cassius or Caesar never shall turn back,°
For I will slay myself.

BRUTUS.   Cassius, be constant.°                                     25
Popilius Lena speaks not of our purposes;
For look, he smiles, and Caesar doth not change.°

CASSIUS.   Trebonius knows his time; for look you, Brutus,
He draws Mark Antony out of the way.
                              [*Exeunt Antony and Trebonius.*]

DECIUS.   Where is Metellus Cimber? Let him go                       30
And presently prefer° his suit to Caesar.

BRUTUS.   He is addressed.° Press near and second him.

CINNA.   Casca, you are the first that rears your hand.

CAESAR.   Are we all ready? What is now amiss
That Caesar and his° Senate must redress?                            35

METELLUS.   Most high, most mighty, and most puissant°
   Caesar,
Metellus Cimber throws before thy seat
An humble heart.                          [*Kneels.*]

CAESAR.   I must prevent thee, Cimber.
These couchings° and these lowly courtesies°                         40
Might fire the blood of ordinary men
And turn preordinance and first decree

---

20 **makes** goes
21 **Casca** Casca is to give the first blow (see 33, 83)
21 **sudden** quick
21 **prevention** i.e. anticipation and discovery
**14-27 I wish . . . change** a further heightening of suspense, since Popilius Lena, although not one of the conspirators, seems to know about the plan
**22-27 Brutus . . . change** Cassius shows here a trace of the excitability and impulsiveness that will be his undoing later when he misreads the state of the battle and kills himself (V iii 34-74), while Brutus shows the reasonableness and composure that will (to some extent) be *his* undoing later, when he faces the Roman populace after the assassination and disdains to rouse them on the conspirators' behalf
23 **turn back** return alive
25 **constant** calm
27 **change** change his expression
31 **presently prefer** immediately present
32 **addressed** ready
35 **his** (a revealing touch)
36 **puissant** powerful
40 **couchings** bows
40 **courtesies** curtsies

Into the law of children.° Be not fond°
To think that Caesar bears such rebel° blood
That° will be thawed° from the true quality°                    45
With that° which melteth fools—I mean, sweet words,
Low-crookèd° curtsies, and base spaniel° fawning.
Thy brother by decree is banishèd.
If thou dost bend and pray and fawn for him,
I spurn thee like a cur out of my way.                          50
Know, Caesar doth not wrong, nor without cause
Will he be satisfied.°

METELLUS.   Is there no voice more worthy than my own,
To sound more sweetly in great Caesar's ear
For the repealing° of my banished brother?                      55

BRUTUS.   I kiss thy hand, but not in flattery, Caesar,
Desiring thee that Publius Cimber may
Have an immediate freedom of repeal.°

CAESAR.   What, Brutus?

CASSIUS.   Pardon, Caesar! Caesar, pardon!                      60
As low as to thy foot doth Cassius fall
To beg enfranchisement° for Publius Cimber.

CAESAR.   I could be well moved, if I were as you;°
If I could pray to move, prayers would move me:°
But I am constant as the Northern Star,°                        65
Of whose true-fixed and resting° quality
There is no fellow° in the firmament.
The skies are painted° with unnumb'red sparks,
They are all fire, and every one doth shine;
But there's but one in all doth hold° his place.               70

---

42-43 **turn . . . children**   make all that has
ever been settled by ordinance and decree
—i.e. the whole fabric of civil life—as capri-
cious as if governed by the law of children
("Law" is Johnson's emendation of the
Folio's "lane")
43 **fond**   so foolish as
44 **rebel**   fickle
45 **That**   as
45 **thawed**   i.e. softened
45 **quality**   i.e. firmness
46 **that**   those things
47 **Low-crookèd**   low-bending (at the knee)
47 **spaniel**   dog-like
52 **satisfied**   i.e. to the point of altering
his decree
55 **repealing**   recalling

58 **freedom of repeal**   release from the decree that prevents his recall
62 **enfranchisment**   freedom
63 **if . . . you**   if I were an ordinary man
(like you)
64 **If . . . me**   if I were weak enough that
I could pray others to change their minds,
then I would also be weak enough that
their prayers would change mine
65 **Northern Star**   Pole   Star   (traditional
symbol of absolute fixity)
66 **resting**   immovable
67 **fellow**   parallel
68 **painted**   adorned
70 **hold**   stay fixed in

So in the world: 'tis furnished well with men,
And men are flesh and blood, and apprehensive;°
Yet in the number I do know but one
That unassailable holds on his rank,
Unshaked of motion;° and that I am he,                          75
Let me a little show it, even in this—
That I was constant Cimber should be banished
And constant° do remain to keep him so.

CINNA.    O Caesar.

CAESAR.    Hence! Wilt thou lift up Olympus?°                    80

DECIUS.    Great Caesar.

CAESAR.    Doth not Brutus bootless kneel?°

CASCA.    Speak hands for me.
                 *They stab Caesar [—Casca first, Brutus last].*

CAESAR.    *Et tu, Brutè?*°—Then fall Caesar.          *Dies.*

CINNA.    Liberty! Freedom! Tyranny is dead!°                    85
Run hence, proclaim, cry it about the streets!

CASSIUS.    Some to the common pulpits° and cry out
"Liberty, freedom, and enfranchisement!"

BRUTUS.    People and senators, be not affrighted.
Fly not; stand still. Ambition's debt° is paid.                 90

CASCA.    Go to the pulpit, Brutus.

DECIUS.    And Cassius too.

BRUTUS.    Where's Publius?°

CINNA.    Here, quite confounded with this mutiny.

---

72  **apprehensive**  quick to react
75  **Unshaked of motion**  not subject to alteration
78  **constant**  fixed in my resolve that
80  **lift up Olympus**  i.e. attempt what no mortal, only Zeus, can perform
82  **Doth . . . kneel**  i.e. when even Brutus, my close friend, petitions me in vain (as in the present case), do you think I will yield to *you*, Decius?
84  *Et tu, Brutè*  You too (even *you*), Brutus? (spoken by Caesar when he realizes that Brutus has stabbed him like the rest)
81-84  **Great . . .**  *Brutè*  an intensely vivid and dramatic scene as all (save Casca) kneel before the god that Caesar at this moment pretends to be and then rise to stab the fallible human being that Caesar actually is

85  **Tyranny is dead**  (perhaps the most ironical remark in the play, since Caesar had so far not shown himself to be a tyrant [see II i 19-21] and his death, as the rest of the play shows, only sets free the tyrannical spirit in Rome)
87  **pulpits**  platforms where public speeches were delivered
90  **debt**  due
93  **Publius**  apparently the senator who enters with the conspirators to escort Caesar to the Capitol (II ii 112 s.d.), but is not privy to their plan and who is now too shocked and confused and enfeebled by age to flee like the rest

METELLUS.    Stand fast together, lest some friend of Caesar's    95
    Should chance—

BRUTUS.    Talk not of standing!° Publius, good cheer.
    There is no harm intended to your person
    Nor to no Roman else. So tell them, Publius.

CASSIUS.    And leave us, Publius, lest that the people,    100
    Rushing on us, should do your age° some mischief.

BRUTUS.    Do so; and let no man abide° this deed
    But we the doers.

               *Enter Trebonius.*

CASSIUS.    Where is Antony?

TREBONIUS.    Fled to his house amazed.°    105
    Men, wives, and children stare, cry out, and run,
    As° it were doomsday.

BRUTUS.    Fates, we will know your pleasures.°
    That we shall die, we know; 'tis but the time,
    And drawing days out, that men stand upon.°    110

CASCA.    Why, he that cuts off twenty years of life
    Cuts off so many years of fearing death.

BRUTUS.    Grant that, and then is death a benefit.
    So are we Caesar's friends, that have abridged
    His time of fearing death. Stoop, Romans, stoop,    115
    And let us bathe our hands in Caesar's blood
    Up to the elbows and besmear our swords.
    Then walk we forth, even to the market place,°
    And waving our red weapons o'er our heads,
    Let's all cry "Peace, freedom, and liberty!"    120

CASSIUS.    Stoop then and wash. How many ages hence
    Shall this our lofty scene be acted over
    In states unborn and accents° yet unknown!

---

**97 standing** organizing physical resistance
**101 your age** i.e. you, an old man
**102 abide** pay for
**105 amazed** dismayed
**107 As** as if
**108 we . . . pleasures** (1) we demand to know (?) (2) we are about to find out (?) —what you have in store

**109-10 time . . . upon** i.e. of course we are to die, for all men must; it is only the particular moment of its arrival and the prolonging of the time before it arrives that men get concerned about
**118 market place** i.e. the Forum
**123 accents** languages

BRUTUS.   How many times shall Caesar bleed in sport,°
That now on Pompey's basis° lies along°                              125
No worthier than the dust!

CASSIUS.   So oft as that shall be,
So often shall the knot° of us be called
The men that gave their country liberty.

DECIUS.   What, shall we forth?                                     130

CASSIUS.   Ay, every man away.
Brutus shall lead, and we will grace° his heels
With the most boldest and best hearts of Rome.

*Enter a Servant.*

BRUTUS.   Soft!° who comes here? A friend of Antony's.

SERVANT.   Thus, Brutus, did my master bid me kneel;°             135
Thus did Mark Antony bid me fall down;
And being prostrate, thus he bade me say:
Brutus is noble, wise, valiant, and honest;
Caesar was mighty, bold, royal, and loving.
Say I love Brutus and I honor him;                                 140
Say I feared Caesar, honored him, and loved him.
If Brutus will vouchsafe that Antony
May safely come to him and be resolved°
How Caesar hath deserved to lie in death,
Mark Antony shall not love Caesar dead                             145
So well as Brutus living; but will follow
The fortunes and affairs of noble Brutus
Thorough° the hazards of this untrod state°
With all true faith. So says my master Antony.

BRUTUS.   Thy master is a wise and valiant Roman.                  150
I never thought him worse.
Tell him, so° please him come° unto this place,
He shall be satisfied and, by my honor,
Depart untouched.

---

124 **in sport** for entertainment (in plays that will be written about him)
125 **Pompey's basis** the base of Pompey's statue
125 **along** stretched out
128 **knot** group (thought of as "bound" together)
132 **grace** do honor to
134 **Soft** wait
135 **kneel** Antony's messenger, kneeling to the conspirators, makes an effective count- erpoint to and commentary on the preceding episode, where the conspirators, pretending a similar awe, knelt before their intended victim
143 **be resolved** be made to understand
148 **Thorough** through
148 **this . . . state** the unknown condition of things that results from Caesar's death
152 **so** if it
152 **come** to come

SERVANT.  I'll fetch him presently.°                              *Exit.*  155

BRUTUS.  I know that we shall have him well to° friend.

CASSIUS.  I wish we may. But yet have I a mind°
That fears him much; and my misgiving still
Falls shrewdly to the purpose.°

*Enter Antony.*

BRUTUS.  But here comes Antony.                                          160
Welcome, Mark Antony.

ANTONY.  O mighty Caesar! dost thou lie so low?
Are all thy conquests, glories, triumphs, spoils,
Shrunk to this little measure? Fare thee well.
I know not, gentlemen, what you intend,                               165
Who else must be let blood, who else is rank.°
If I myself, there is no hour so fit
As Caesar's death's hour; nor no instrument
Of half that worth as those your swords, made rich
With the most noble blood of all this world.                          170
I do beseech ye, if you bear me hard,°
Now, whilst your purpled° hands do reek and smoke,°
Fulfil your pleasure. Live° a thousand years,
I shall not find myself so apt° to die;
No place will please me so, no mean° of death,                        175
As here by Caesar,° and by you cut off,
The choice and master spirits of this age.°

BRUTUS.  O Antony, beg not your death of us!
Though now we must appear bloody and cruel,

---

155 **presently** immediately
156 **to** as a
157 **mind** presentiment
158-59 **my . . . purpose** my misgivings
always come close to the truth (see Caesar's
comment, I ii 214-15)
166 **Who . . . rank** "Let blood" refers to
the former medical practice of drawing off
a portion of a patient's blood to cure him
of excess and "rank" refers to the horticul-
tural practice of cutting back a too luxuriant
or aggressive plant. By putting forward ironically these euphemisms for what was in
fact a murder—euphemisms very similar to
those by which the murderers intend to
justify their violent act as beneficent and
sacrificial—Antony reduces them in advance
to absurdity and gives a foretaste of the
strategy by which he will soon reduce the
proposition that "Brutus is an honorable
man" (III ii 80ff)

171 **bear me hard** see note I ii 323
172 **purpled** bloodied
172 **reek and smoke** i.e. like priests'
hands after cutting the throats of sacrificial
animals at the altar (Antony again, with
deliberate irony, pretends to fall in with
the idea that the murder was a sacrifice,
but promptly undercuts it with "Fulfil your
pleasure")
173 **Live** if I should live
174 **so apt** i.e. a moment in which I shall
feel so ready
175 **mean** means
176 **by Caesar** beside Caesar
171-77 **I do . . . age** Antony shows himself a master at role-playing; not for
nothing is he so fond of the theater (I ii
215-16)

As by our hands and this our present act                    180
You see we do, yet see you but our hands
And this the bleeding business they have done.
Our hearts you see not. They are pitiful;°
And pity to the general wrong of Rome
(As fire drives out fire, so pity pity)°                    185
Hath done this deed on Caesar. For your part,
To you our swords have leaden° points, Mark Antony.
Our arms in strength of malice, and our hearts
Of brothers' temper,° do receive you in
With all kind love, good thoughts, and reverence.          190

CASSIUS.   Your voice° shall be as strong as any man's
In the disposing of new dignities.°

BRUTUS.   Only be patient till we have appeased
The multitude, beside themselves with fear,
And then we will deliver° you the cause                     195
Why I, that did love Caesar when I struck him,
Have thus proceeded.

ANTONY.   I doubt not of your wisdom.
Let each man render me his bloody hand.
First, Marcus Brutus, will I shake with you;               200
Next, Caius Cassius, do I take your hand;
Now, Decius Brutus, yours; now yours, Metellus;
Yours, Cinna; and, my valiant Casca, yours.
Though last, not least in love, yours, good Trebonius.
Gentlemen all—Alas, what shall I say?                       205
My credit° now stands on such slippery ground
That one of two bad ways you must conceit° me,
Either a coward or a flatterer.
That I did love thee, Caesar, O, 'tis true!
If then thy spirit look upon us now,                        210
Shall it not grieve thee dearer° than thy death
To see thy Antony making his peace,
Shaking the bloody fingers of thy foes,

---

183  **pitiful**  full of pity
185  **pity pity**  i.e. pity for the people of
Rome overcame pity for Caesar
187  **leaden**  blunted
188-89  **Our . . . temper**  i.e. our arms, with
a strength that only looks hostile, and our
hearts with an affection that is truly
brotherly
191  **voice**  vote

192  **dignities**  offices
191-92  **Your . . . dignities**  Cassius, always
a keen judge of men, hastens to arguments
likely to be more persuasive with Antony
than Brutus's
195  **deliver**  tell
206  **credit**  reputation
207  **conceit**  regard
211  **dearer**  yet more

Most noble!° in the presence of thy corpse?
Had I as many eyes as thou hast wounds,                              215
Weeping as fast as they stream forth thy blood,
It° would become me better than to close°
In terms of friendship with thine enemies.
Pardon me, Julius! Here wast thou bayed,° brave hart;°
Here didst thou fall; and here thy hunters stand,°              220
Signed in thy spoil,° and crimsoned in thy lethe.°
O world, thou wast the forest to this hart;
And this indeed, O world, the heart of thee!
How like a deer, stroken° by many princes,
Dost thou here lie!                                                  225

CASSIUS.    Mark Antony—

ANTONY.    Pardon me, Caius Cassius.
The enemies of Caesar shall say this;°
Then, in a friend, it is cold modesty.°

CASSIUS.    I blame you not for praising Caesar so;              230
But what compact mean you to have with us?
Will you be pricked° in number of our friends,
Or shall we on,° and not depend on you?

ANTONY.    Therefore I took your hands, but was indeed
Swayed from the point by looking down on Caesar.               235
Friends am I with you all, and love you all,
Upon this hope, that you shall give me reasons
Why and wherein Caesar was dangerous.

BRUTUS.    Or else were this° a savage spectacle.
Our reasons are so full of good regard°                           240
That were you, Antony, the son of Caesar,
You should be satisfied.

---

214 **Most noble** (1) spoken sarcastically of
his own act in shaking hands (?)  (2) spoken
passionately of his dead friend Caesar (?)
217 **It** i.e. to mourn
217 **close** join
219 **bayed** brought to bay
219 **hart** deer (with pun on "heart")
219-20 **Pardon . . . stand** Antony here
shifts our sense of the assassination from a
priestly act performed on a sacrificial victim (Brutus's interpretation: II i 180) to an
act of hunters who have brought down a
noble prey—an interpretation that Brutus
has explicitly resisted (II i 181)

221 **Signed . . . spoil** marked with signs
of your ruin
221 **lethe** death, i.e. the bloody action
which brought you to oblivion (Lethe is the
underworld river of forgetfulness)
224 **stroken** struck
228 **this** i.e. as much as this
229 **modesty** moderation
232 **pricked** listed (literally, to prick a
name is to mark it with a dot)
233 **on** go on
239 **Or . . . this** otherwise this would be
240 **regard** reason

ANTONY.    That's all I seek;
And am moreover suitor that I may
Produce° his body to the market place                                   245
And in the pulpit, as becomes° a friend,
Speak in the order° of his funeral.

BRUTUS.    You shall, Mark Antony.

CASSIUS.    Brutus, a word with you.
[*Aside to Brutus*] You know not what you do. Do not   250
consent
That Antony speak in his funeral.°
Know you how much the people may be moved
By that which he will utter?

BRUTUS.    [*aside to Cassius*] By your pardon—
I will myself into the pulpit first                                     255
And show the reason of our Caesar's death.
What Antony shall speak, I will protest°
He speaks by leave and by permission;
And that we are contented Caesar shall
Have all true° rites and lawful ceremonies.                            260
It shall advantage more than do us wrong.

CASSIUS.    [*aside to Brutus*] I know not what may fall.° I like it
not.

BRUTUS.    Mark Antony, here, take you Caesar's body.
You shall not in your funeral speech blame us,
But speak all good you can devise of Caesar;                            265
And say you do't by our permission.
Else shall you not have any hand at all
About his funeral. And you shall speak
In the same pulpit whereto I am going,
After my speech is ended.                                              270

ANTONY.    Be it so.
I do desire no more.

BRUTUS.    Prepare the body then, and follow us.

                                        *Exeunt. Manet Antony.*

---

245  **Produce**  bring forth
246  **becomes**  is fitting for
247  **order**  ceremony
250-51  **You . . . funeral**  Shakespeare
stresses again that Cassius knows the man
they are dealing with

257  **protest**  declare
260  **true**  due
262  **fall**  happen

ANTONY.  O, pardon me, thou bleeding piece of earth,
That I am meek and gentle with these butchers!°                        275
Thou art the ruins of the noblest man
That ever livèd in the tide of times.°
Woe to the hand that shed this costly° blood!
Over thy wounds now do I prophesy
(Which, like dumb mouths, do ope their ruby lips                       280
To beg the voice and utterance of my tongue),
A curse shall light upon the limbs of men;
Domestic fury and fierce civil strife
Shall cumber° all the parts of Italy;
Blood and destruction shall be so in use                               285
And dreadful objects so familiar
That mothers shall but smile when they behold
Their infants quarterèd with the hands of war,
All pity choked with custom of° fell° deeds;
And Caesar's spirit, ranging° for revenge,                             290
With Atè° by his side come hot from hell,
Shall in these confines° with a monarch's voice
Cry "Havoc!"° and let slip° the dogs of war,
That° this foul deed shall smell above the earth
With carrion° men, groaning for burial.                                295

*Enter Octavius' Servant.*

You serve Octavius Caesar, do you not?

SERVANT.  I do, Mark Antony.

ANTONY.  Caesar did write for him to come to Rome.

SERVANT.  He did receive his letters and is coming,
And bid me say to you by word of mouth—                                300
O Caesar!

ANTONY.  Thy heart is big.° Get thee apart° and weep.
Passion, I see, is catching;° for mine eyes,

---

275 **butchers** (Antony no longer speaks of sacrificers, or even hunters)
277 **tide of times** course of history
278 **costly** (1) valuable (see 170) (2) requiring to be paid for by those who shed it
284 **cumber** trouble
289 **with . . . of** because accustomed to
289 **fell** savage
290 **ranging** roving like a beast searching for its prey
291 **Atè** goddess of discord

292 **confines** regions
293 **Havoc** the signal for uncontrolled massacre and pillage
293 **let slip** unleash
294 **That** i.e. until
295 **carrion** rotting
302 **big** (with grief)
302 **apart** off by yourself
303 **Passion . . . catching** (an observation that Antony will soon apply in practice when arousing the populace's feelings through his own)

Seeing those beads of sorrow stand in thine,
Began to water. Is thy master coming?                    305

SERVANT.  He lies to-night within seven leagues of Rome.

ANTONY.  Post° back with speed
And tell him what hath chanced.
Here is a mourning Rome, a dangerous Rome,
No Rome° of safety for Octavius yet.                     310
Hie° hence and tell him so. Yet stay awhile.
Thou shalt not back till I have borne this corpse
Into the market place. There shall I try°
In my oration how the people take
The cruel issue° of these bloody men;                    315
According to the which thou shalt discourse
To young Octavius of the state of things.
Lend me your hand.          *Exeunt [with Caesar's body].*

*Enter Brutus and [presently] goes into the*            III ii
*pulpit, and Cassius, with the Plebeians.*

PLEBEIANS.  We will be satisfied!° Let us be satisfied!

BRUTUS.  Then follow me and give me audience, friends.
Cassius, go you into the other street
And part the numbers.°
Those that will hear me speak, let 'em stay here;        5
Those that will follow Cassius, go with him;
And public reasons shall be renderèd°
Of Caesar's death.

1. PLEBEIAN.  I will hear Brutus speak.

---

307  **Post** hasten
310  **Rome** (see note I ii 166)
311  **Hie** hurry
313  **try** test
315  **issue** result
**III ii 1 will be satisfied** demand a complete explanation

4  **part the numbers** divide the crowd
7  **public . . . renderèd** (1) reasons shall be rendered publicly (?) (2) reasons shall be rendered that concern the public welfare (?)

2. PLEBEIAN.   I will hear Cassius, and compare their reasons    10
When severally° we hear them renderèd.

[*Exit Cassius, with some of the Plebeians.*]

3. PLEBEIAN.   The noble Brutus is ascended. Silence!

BRUTUS.   Be patient till the last.°
Romans, countrymen, and lovers,° hear me for my cause,
and be silent, that you may hear. Believe me for mine    15
honor, and have respect to° mine honor, that you may
believe. Censure° me in your wisdom, and awake your
senses,° that you may the better judge. If there be any in
this assembly, any dear friend of Caesar's, to him I say that
Brutus' love to Caesar was no less than his. If then that    20
friend demand why Brutus rose against Caesar, this is my
answer: Not that I loved Caesar less, but that I loved Rome
more. Had you rather Caesar were living, and die all slaves,
than that Caesar were dead, to live all freemen? As Caesar
loved me, I weep for him; as he was fortunate, I rejoice at    25
it; as he was valiant, I honor him; but—as he was ambitious, I slew him. There is tears for his love; joy for his
fortune; honor for his valor; and death for his ambition.
Who is here so base that would be a bondman?° If any,
speak; for him have I offended. Who is here so rude° that    30
would not be a Roman? If any, speak; for him have I
offended. Who is here so vile that will not love his country? If any, speak; for him have I offended. I pause for a
reply.

ALL.   None, Brutus, none!    35

BRUTUS.   Then none have I offended. I have done no more to
Caesar than you shall do° to Brutus. The question° of his
death is enrolled in the Capitol;° his glory not extenuated,°
wherein he was worthy; nor his offenses enforced,° for
which he suffered death.    40

*Enter Mark Antony [and others], with Caesar's body.*

---

11  **severally**  separately
13  **last**  conclusion
14  **lovers**  dear friends
16  **have . . . to**  give due consideration to
17  **Censure**  judge
18  **senses**  intellectual powers
29  **bondman**  slave
30  **rude**  barbarous

37  **you . . . do**  I invite you to do to me
(if I should become as tyrannical as Caesar)
37  **question**  story
38  **enrolled . . . Capitol**  i.e. already set
down in the state archives
38  **extenuated**  belittled
39  **enforced**  exaggerated

Here comes his body, mourned by Mark Antony, who,
though he had no hand in his death, shall receive the benefit of his dying, a place° in the commonwealth, as which
of you shall not? With this° I depart, that, as I slew my
best lover° for the good of Rome, I have the same dagger  45
for myself when it shall please my country to need my
death.

ALL.    Live, Brutus! live, live!

1. PLEBEIAN.    Bring him with triumph home unto his house.

2. PLEBEIAN.°    Give him a statue with his ancestors.                 50

3. PLEBEIAN.    Let him be Caesar.

4. PLEBEIAN.    Caesar's better parts°
Shall be crowned in Brutus.

1. PLEBEIAN.    We'll bring him to his house
With shouts and clamors.°                                              55

BRUTUS.    My countrymen—

2. PLEBEIAN.    Peace! silence! Brutus speaks.

1. PLEBEIAN.    Peace, ho!

BRUTUS.    Good countrymen, let me depart alone,
And, for my sake, stay here with Antony.                              60
Do grace° to Caesar's corpse, and grace his speech
Tending° to Caesar's glories which Mark Antony,
By our permission, is allowed to make.
I do entreat you, not a man depart,
Save I alone, till Antony have spoke.                    *Exit.*  65

1. PLEBEIAN.    Stay, ho! and let us hear Mark Antony.

3. PLEBEIAN.    Let him go up into the public chair.°
We'll hear him. Noble Antony, go up.

ANTONY.    For Brutus' sake I am beholding° to you.

                              [*Antony goes into the pulpit.*]

4. PLEBEIAN.    What does he say of Brutus?                           70

---

43 **place** i.e. as a free citizen of the republic rather than as a slave to Caesar in a
monarchy
44 **this** this statement
45 **lover** friend
50 **2. Plebeian** (this is of course a different member of the crowd from the 2.
Plebeian who went to hear Cassius earlier)

52 **parts** qualities
48-55 **Live . . . clamors** The responses of
the crowd to Brutus's speech show how
little they understand him and his motives
61 **Do grace** show respect
62 **Tending** relating
67 **chair** pulpit
69 **beholding** beholden, i.e. obliged

3. PLEBEIAN.    He says for Brutus' sake
        He finds himself beholding to us all.

4. PLEBEIAN.    'Twere best he speak no harm of Brutus here!

1. PLEBEIAN.    This Caesar was a tyrant.

3. PLEBEIAN.    Nay, that's certain.                                          75
        We are blest that Rome is rid of him.

2. PLEBEIAN.    Peace! Let us hear what Antony can say.

ANTONY.    You gentle Romans—

ALL.    Peace, ho! Let us hear him.

ANTONY.    Friends, Romans, countrymen, lend me your ears;        80
        I come to bury Caesar, not to praise him.
        The evil that men do lives after them;°
        The good is oft interrèd with their bones.
        So let it be with Caesar. The noble Brutus
        Hath told you Caesar was ambitious.                              85
        If it were so, it was a grievous fault,
        And grievously hath Caesar answered° it.
        Here under leave of Brutus and the rest
        (For Brutus is an honorable man;
        So are they all, all honorable men),                             90
        Come I to speak in Caesar's funeral.
        He was my friend, faithful and just to me;
        But Brutus says he was ambitious,
        And Brutus is an honorable man.
        He hath brought many captives home to Rome,                      95
        Whose ransoms did the general coffers° fill.°
        Did this in Caesar seem ambitious?
        When that the poor have cried, Caesar hath wept;
        Ambition should be made of sterner stuff.
        Yet Brutus says he was ambitious;                               100
        And Brutus is an honorable man.
        You all did see that on the Lupercal
        I thrice presented him a kingly crown,
        Which he did thrice refuse. Was this ambition?
        Yet Brutus says he was ambitious;                               105
        And sure he is an honorable man.

---

**82  after them**  i.e. in men's memories
**87  answered**  answered for

**95-96  He . . . fill**  Antony carefully neglects to mention the aspect of Caesar's rise that we were shown in I i, especially 32-5
**96  general coffers**  public treasury

> I speak not to disprove what Brutus spoke,
> But here I am to speak what I do know.
> You all did love him once, not without cause.
> What cause withholds you then to mourn for him?                    110
> O judgment, thou art fled to brutish beasts,
> And men have lost their reason!° Bear with me.°
> My heart is in the coffin there with Caesar,
> And I must pause till it come back to me.

1. PLEBEIAN.   Methinks there is much reason in his sayings.         115

2. PLEBEIAN.   If thou consider rightly of the matter,
> Caesar has had great wrong.

3. PLEBEIAN.   Has he, masters? I fear there will a worse come
> in his place.°

4. PLEBEIAN.   Marked ye his words? He would not take the
> crown;
> Therefore 'tis certain he was not ambitious.                       120

1. PLEBEIAN.   If it be found so, some will dear abide it.°

2. PLEBEIAN.   Poor soul! his eyes are red as fire with weeping.

3. PLEBEIAN.   There's not a nobler man in Rome than Antony.

4. PLEBEIAN.   Now mark him. He begins again to speak.

ANTONY.   But° yesterday the word of Caesar might                    125
> Have stood against the world. Now lies he there,
> And none so poor to do° him reverence.
> O masters! If I were disposed to stir
> Your hearts and minds to mutiny and rage,
> I should do Brutus wrong, and Cassius wrong,                       130
> Who, you all know, are honorable men.
> I will not do them wrong. I rather choose
> To wrong the dead, to wrong myself and you,
> Than I will wrong such honorable men.
> But here's a parchment with the seal of Caesar.                    135
> I found it in his closet;° 'tis his will.
> Let but the commons hear this testament,

---

111-12 **O . . . reason** i.e. since any man
who *could* reason would surely grieve for a
benefactor, and you don't, the only explanation must be that the capacity to reason
has descended from man's rank in the scale
of being to the beasts' rank
112 **Bear with me** (Antony's voice has
broken with emotion in 111-12)

117-18 **Caesar . . . place** Some editors re-
lineate *Caesar . . . masters?/I . . . place*
121 **dear . . . it**  pay dearly for it
125 **But**  only
127 **to do**  as to do
136 **closet**  private apartment

Which (pardon me) I do not mean to read,
And they would go and kiss dead Caesar's wounds
And dip their napkins° in his sacred blood;                      140
Yea, beg a hair of him for memory,
And dying, mention it within their wills,
Bequeathing it as a rich legacy
Unto their issue.°

4. PLEBEIAN.    We'll hear the will! Read it, Mark Antony.        145

ALL.    The will, the will! We will hear Caesar's will!

ANTONY.    Have patience, gentle friends; I must not read it.
It is not meet° you know how Caesar loved you.
You are not wood, you are not stones, but men;
And being men, hearing the will of Caesar,                       150
It will inflame you, it will make you mad.°
'Tis good you know not that you are his heirs;
For if you should, O, what would come of it?

4. PLEBEIAN.    Read the will! We'll hear it, Antony!
You shall read us the will, Caesar's will!                       155

ANTONY.    Will you be patient? Will you stay° awhile?
I have o'ershot myself° to tell you of it.
I fear I wrong the honorable men
Whose daggers have stabbed Caesar; I do fear it.

4. PLEBEIAN.    They were traitors. Honorable men!               160

ALL.    The will! the testament!

2. PLEBEIAN.    They were villains, murderers! The will! Read the
will!

ANTONY.    You will compel me then to read the will?
Then make a ring about the corpse of Caesar                      165
And let me show you him that made the will.
Shall I descend? and will you give me leave?

ALL.    Come down.

2. PLEBEIAN.    Descend.

3. PLEBEIAN.    You shall have leave.        [*Antony comes down.*]  170

---

140 **napkins** handkerchiefs
144 **issue** heirs
140-44 **And dip . . . issue** Antony's version of the martyrdom first described by
Decius (II ii 90-94)

148 **meet** fitting
151 **mad** crazed
156 **stay** wait
157 **o'ershot myself** o'ershot the mark,
i.e. gone too far

4. PLEBEIAN.    A ring! Stand round.

1. PLEBEIAN.    Stand from the hearse!° Stand from the body!

2. PLEBEIAN.    Room for Antony, most noble Antony!

ANTONY.    Nay, press not so upon me. Stand far° off.

ALL.    Stand back! Room! Bear back!                                    175

ANTONY.    If you have tears, prepare to shed them now.
You all do know this mantle. I remember
The first time ever Caesar put it on.
'Twas on a summer's evening in his tent,
That day he overcame the Nervii.°                                      180
Look, in this place ran Cassius' dagger through.
See what a rent the envious° Casca made.
Through this the well-belovèd Brutus stabbed;
And as he plucked his cursèd steel away,
Mark how the blood of Caesar followed it,                              185
As° rushing out of doors to be resolved°
If Brutus so unkindly° knocked or no;
For Brutus, as you know, was Caesar's angel.°
Judge, O you gods, how dearly Caesar loved him!
This was the most unkindest° cut of all;                               190
For when the noble Caesar saw him stab,
Ingratitude, more strong than traitors' arms,
Quite vanquished him. Then burst his mighty heart;
And in his mantle muffling up his face,
Even at the base of Pompey's statue                                    195
(Which all the while ran blood°) great Caesar fell.°
O, what a fall was there, my countrymen!
Then I, and you, and all of us fell down,
Whilst bloody treason flourished over us.
O, now you weep, and I perceive you feel                               200

---

172   **hearse** bier
174   **far** farther
180   **Nervii** Gallic tribe defeated in 57 B.C.
182   **envious** malicious
186   **As** as though
186   **resolved** certain
187   **unkindly** (1) unnaturally   (2) cruelly
188   **angel** favorite
190   **most unkindest** most unnatural and cruel
196   **Which . . . blood** Antony must mean to imply that Pompey sympathizes with Caesar, but Shakespeare may have meant his audience to remember the tradition that a murdered man bleeds afresh in the pres-

ence of his murderer, i.e. that in Caesar's death Pompey's is revenged
181-96   **Look . . . fell** We must suppose (1) that Shakespeare here forgets that Antony did not witness the assassination, or—which is hardly plausible—(2) that there was time between III i and III ii for Antony to learn just these circumstances and map out the corpse like a problem in geometry, or—which is much more plausible—(3) that like most oratorical spellbinders, Antony fictionalizes—he cannot actually know from observation which dagger went where or that Caesar muffled up his face (194)

The dint° of pity. These are gracious drops.
Kind souls, what° weep you when you but behold
Our Caesar's vesture° wounded? Look you here!
Here is himself, marred as you see with° traitors.

1. PLEBEIAN.    O piteous spectacle!                                   205

2. PLEBEIAN.    O noble Caesar!

3. PLEBEIAN.    O woeful day!

4. PLEBEIAN.    O traitors, villains!

1. PLEBEIAN.    O most bloody sight!

2. PLEBEIAN.    We will be revenged.                                   210

[ALL.]    Revenge! About!° Seek! Burn! Fire! Kill! Slay!
Let not a traitor live!

ANTONY.    Stay, countrymen.

1. PLEBEIAN.    Peace there! Hear the noble Antony.

2. PLEBEIAN.    We'll hear him, we'll follow him, we'll die with   215
him!

ANTONY.    Good friends, sweet friends, let me not stir you up
To such a sudden flood of mutiny.
They that have done this deed are honorable.
What private griefs° they have, alas, I know not,               220
That made them do it. They are wise and honorable,
And will no doubt with reasons answer you.
I come not, friends, to steal away your hearts.
I am no orator, as Brutus is,
But (as you know me all) a plain blunt man                      225
That love my friend; and that they know full well
That gave me public leave to speak of him.
For I have neither wit, nor words, nor worth,
Action, nor utterance, nor the power of speech
To stir men's blood.° I only speak right on.°                   230
I tell you that which you yourselves do know,

---

201 **dint** stroke
202 **what** why
203 **vesture** clothing
204 **with** by
211 **About** i.e. let's be about it
220 **griefs** grievances (Antony represents the conspirators' motives as private grudges, not public concern)
230 **right on** without premeditation

228-30 **wit . . . blood** Antony here summarizes the virtues of the ideal orator: "wit" is the invention that finds out good arguments, which must then be clothed in proper "words" and spoken with authority (the orator's "worth" or ethos), accompanied by the "action" of fit gestures, by skillful elocution ("utterance"), and by the capacity (that certain thrilling voices have) to "stir men's blood"

Show you sweet Caesar's wounds, poor poor dumb mouths,
And bid them speak for me. But were I Brutus,
And Brutus Antony, there were an Antony
Would ruffle up° your spirits, and put a tongue                    235
In every wound of Caesar that should move
The stones of Rome to rise and mutiny.

ALL.    We'll mutiny.

1. PLEBEIAN.    We'll burn the house of Brutus.

3. PLEBEIAN.    Away then! Come, seek the conspirators.             240

ANTONY.    Yet hear me, countrymen. Yet hear me speak.

ALL.    Peace, ho! Hear Antony, most noble Antony.

ANTONY.    Why, friends, you go to do you know not what.
Wherein hath Caesar thus deserved your loves?
Alas, you know not! I must tell you then.                          245
You have forgot the will I told you of.

ALL.    Most true! The will! Let's stay and hear the will.

ANTONY.    Here is the will, and under Caesar's seal.
To every Roman citizen he gives,
To every several° man, seventy-five drachmas.°                     250

2. PLEBEIAN.    Most noble Caesar! We'll revenge his death!

3. PLEBEIAN.    O royal° Caesar!

ANTONY.    Hear me with patience.

ALL.    Peace, ho!

ANTONY.    Moreover, he hath left you all his walks,°              255
His private arbors, and new-planted orchards,°
On this side Tiber; he hath left them you,
And to your heirs for ever—common pleasures,°
To walk abroad and recreate yourselves.
Here was a Caesar! When comes such another?                        260

1. PLEBEIAN.    Never, never! Come, away, away!
We'll burn his body in the holy place
And with the brands fire the traitors' houses.
Take up the body.

---

235 **ruffle up** arouse
250 **several** individual
250 **seventy-five drachmas** (a substantial bequest in the eyes of men who had nothing)

252 **royal** regal in generosity
255 **walks** parks
256 **orchards** gardens
258 **pleasures** i.e. pleasure-gardens

2. PLEBEIAN.　Go fetch fire!　　　　　　　　　　　　　　265

3. PLEBEIAN.　Pluck down benches!

4. PLEBEIAN.　Pluck down forms,° windows,° anything!
　　　　　　　　　　*Exit Plebeians [with the body].*

ANTONY.　Now let it work. Mischief, thou art afoot,
　　Take thou what course thou wilt.
　　　　　　　　　*Enter Servant.*

　　How now, fellow?　　　　　　　　　　　　　　270

SERVANT.　Sir, Octavius is already come to Rome.

ANTONY.　Where is he?

SERVANT.　He and Lepidus are at Caesar's house.

ANTONY.　And thither will I straight° to visit him.
　　He comes upon a wish.° Fortune is merry,　　　　275
　　And in this mood will give us anything.

SERVANT.　I heard him say Brutus and Cassius
　　Are rid° like madmen through the gates of Rome.

ANTONY.　Belike° they had some notice of° the people,
　　How I had moved them. Bring me to Octavius.　　*Exeunt.* 280

❧～❧～❧

*Enter Cinna the Poet, and after him the Plebeians.*　　　III iii

CINNA.　I dreamt to-night° that I did feast with Caesar,
　　And things unluckily charge my fantasy.°
　　I have no will to wander forth° of doors,
　　Yet something leads me forth.

1. PLEBEIAN.　What is your name?　　　　　　　　　5

2. PLEBEIAN.　Whither are you going?

3. PLEBEIAN.　Where do you dwell?

---

267　**forms** benches
267　**windows** shutters
274　**straight** immediately
275　**upon a wish** as I wished
278　**Are rid** have ridden
279　**Belike** probably

279　**notice of** news concerning
**III iii 1　to-night** see note II ii 81
2　**things . . . fantasy** i.e. events make my
dream ominous
3　**forth** out

4. PLEBEIAN.   Are you a married man or a bachelor?

2. PLEBEIAN.   Answer every man directly.°

1. PLEBEIAN.   Ay, and briefly.                                        10

4. PLEBEIAN.   Ay, and wisely.

3. PLEBEIAN.   Ay, and truly, you were best.

CINNA.   What is my name? Whither am I going? Where do I
dwell? Am I a married man or a bachelor? Then, to
answer every man directly and briefly, wisely and truly:   15
wisely I say, I am a bachelor.

2. PLEBEIAN.   That's as much as to say they are fools that
marry. You'll bear me a bang° for that, I fear. Proceed
directly.

CINNA.   Directly I am going to Caesar's funeral.               20

1. PLEBEIAN.   As a friend or an enemy?

CINNA.   As a friend.

2. PLEBEIAN.   That matter is answered directly.

4. PLEBEIAN.   For your dwelling—briefly.

CINNA.   Briefly, I dwell by the Capitol.                          25

3. PLEBEIAN.   Your name, sir, truly.

CINNA.   Truly, my name is Cinna.

1. PLEBEIAN.   Tear him to pieces! He's a conspirator.

CINNA.   I am Cinna the poet! I am Cinna the poet!

4. PLEBEIAN.   Tear him for his bad verses! Tear him for his bad   30
verses!

CINNA.   I am not Cinna the conspirator.

4. PLEBEIAN.   It is no matter; his name's Cinna! Pluck but his
name out of his heart, and turn him going.°

3. PLEBEIAN.   Tear him, tear him! [*They kill him.*] Come,   35
brands,° ho! firebrands! To Brutus', to Cassius'! Burn all!
Some to Decius' house and some to Casca's; some to
Ligarius'! Away, go!
*Exeunt all the Plebeians* [*with the body of Cinna*].

---

9 **directly** i.e. with no nonsense or quibbling
18 **bear me a bang** get a blow from me

34 **turn him going** send him away
36 **brands** torches

※~~※~~※

*Enter Antony, Octavius, and Lepidus.*　　　　　IV i

ANTONY. These many, then, shall die; their names are
　　pricked.°

OCTAVIUS. Your brother too must die. Consent you, Lepidus?

LEPIDUS. I do consent—

OCTAVIUS. Prick him down, Antony.

LEPIDUS. Upon condition Publius shall not live,　　　　　　5
　　Who is your sister's son, Mark Antony.

ANTONY. He shall not live. Look, with a spot° I damn° him.
　　But, Lepidus, go you to Caesar's house.
　　Fetch the will hither, and we shall determine
　　How to cut off some charge in° legacies.　　　　　　　10

LEPIDUS. What? shall I find you here?

OCTAVIUS. Or° here or at the Capitol.　　　　　*Exit Lepidus.*

ANTONY. This is a slight unmeritable man,
　　Meet° to be sent on errands. Is it fit,
　　The threefold° world divided, he should stand　　　　15
　　One of the three to share it?

OCTAVIUS. So you thought him,
　　And took his voice° who should be pricked to die
　　In our black sentence and proscription.°

ANTONY. Octavius, I have seen more days than you;　　　　20
　　And though we lay these honors on this man
　　To ease ourselves of divers sland'rous loads,°
　　He shall but bear them as the ass bears gold,
　　To groan and sweat under the business,
　　Either led or driven as we point the way;　　　　　　25
　　And having brought our treasure where we will,
　　Then take we down his load, and turn him off

---

IV i 1 **pricked** see note III i 232
7 **spot** mark
7 **damn** condemn
10 **cut . . . charge in** reduce some of the
expense of
12 **Or** either

14 **Meet** fit
15 **threefold** i.e. Europe, Africa, Asia
18 **voice** vote
19 **proscription** condemnation
22 **ease . . . loads** i.e. unload on him
some of the censure we shall receive

(Like to the empty ass) to shake his ears
And graze in commons.°

OCTAVIUS.　You may do your will;　　　　　　　　　30
But he's a tried and valiant soldier.

ANTONY.　So is my horse, Octavius, and for that
I do appoint° him store° of provender.°
It is a creature that I teach to fight,
To wind,° to stop, to run directly° on,　　　　　35
His corporal° motion governed by my spirit.
And, in some taste,° is Lepidus but so.
He must be taught, and trained, and bid go forth:
A barren-spirited fellow; one that feeds
On objects, arts, and imitations°　　　　　　　40
Which, out of use and staled° by other men,
Begin° his fashion. Do not talk of him
But as a property.° And now, Octavius,
Listen° great things. Brutus and Cassius
Are levying powers.° We must straight make head.°　45
Therefore let our alliance be combined,
Our best friends made,° our means stretched;°
And let us presently° go sit in council
How° covert matters° may be best disclosed
And open perils surest answerèd.　　　　　　　50

OCTAVIUS.　Let us do so; for we are at the stake°
And bayed about with many enemies;
And some that smile have in their hearts, I fear,
Millions of mischiefs.　　　　　　　*Exeunt.*

| | |
|---|---|
| **29　commons**　public pasture | **44　Listen**　listen to |
| **33　appoint**　allot | **45　levying powers**　raising armies |
| **33　store**　supply | **45　straight . . . head**　immediately raise |
| **33　provender**　food | an army |
| **35　wind**　wheel | **47　made**　mustered |
| **35　directly**　immediately | **47　stretched**　planned so as to stretch to |
| **36　corporal**　bodily | the maximum |
| **37　taste**　measure | **48　presently**　immediately |
| **40　objects . . . limitations**　i.e. curiosities, | **49　How**　to decide how |
| affectations, and clichés | **49　covert matters**　hidden dangers |
| **41　staled**　vulgarized | **51　at the stake**　like a bear tied to a stake |
| **42　Begin**　i.e. become | and surrounded by dogs |
| **43　property**　tool | |

*Drum. Enter Brutus, Lucilius, [Lucius,] and
the Army. Titinius and Pindarus meet them.*

BRUTUS.　Stand ho!

LUCILIUS.　Give the word, ho! and stand!°

BRUTUS.　What now, Lucilius? Is Cassius near?

LUCILIUS.　He is at hand, and Pindarus is come
　　To do you salutation from his master.　　　　　　　　　　5

BRUTUS.　He greets me well.° Your master, Pindarus,
　　In his own change, or by ill officers,°
　　Hath given me some worthy° cause to wish
　　Things done undone; but if he be at hand,
　　I shall be satisfied.°　　　　　　　　　　　　　　　　　10

PINDARUS.　I do not doubt
　　But that my noble master will appear
　　Such as he is, full of regard° and honor.

BRUTUS.　He is not doubted. A word, Lucilius,
　　How he received you. Let me be resolved.°　　　　　　　15

LUCILIUS.　With courtesy and with respect enough,
　　But not with such familiar instances°
　　Nor with such free and friendly conference°
　　As he hath used of old.

BRUTUS.　Thou hast described　　　　　　　　　　　　　20
　　A hot friend cooling. Ever° note, Lucilius,
　　When love begins to sicken and decay
　　It useth an enforcèd ceremony.°
　　There are no tricks° in plain and simple faith;°
　　But hollow° men, like horses hot at hand,°　　　　　　25
　　Make gallant show and promise of their mettle;°
　　　　　　　　　　　　　　*Low march within.*°
　　But when they should endure the bloody spur,

---

IV ii 2　**Give . . . stand** Lucilius passes on
Brutus's command
**6 greets me well** i.e. by sending a worthy
man
**7 In . . . officers** i.e. either because he
has himself changed or because his sub-
ordinates have misbehaved
**8 worthy** fitting
**10 be satisfied** receive an explanation
**13 regard** concern
**15 resolved** fully informed

**17 familiar instances** proofs of friendship
**18 conference** talk
**21 Ever** always
**23 enforcèd ceremony** forced courtesy
**24 tricks** pretenses
**24 faith** love
**25 hollow** insincere
**25 hot at hand** spirited at the outset
**26 mettle** spirit
**26 s.d. Low . . . within** i.e. low sound of
drumbeats offstage

They fall° their crests,° and like deceitful jades°
Sink° in the trial. Comes his army on?

LUCILIUS.    They mean this night in Sardis° to be quartered.     30
The greater part, the horse in general,°
Are come with Cassius.

BRUTUS.    Hark! He is arrived.
March gently° on to meet him.°

*Enter Cassius and his Powers.*

CASSIUS.    Stand, ho!                                            35

BRUTUS.    Stand, ho! Speak the word along.

1. SOLDIER.    Stand!

2. SOLDIER.    Stand!

3. SOLDIER.    Stand!

CASSIUS.    Most noble brother, you have done me wrong.          40

BRUTUS.    Judge me, you gods! wrong I mine enemies?
And if not so, how should I wrong a brother?

CASSIUS.    Brutus, this sober form° of yours hides wrongs;
And when you do them—

BRUTUS.    Cassius, be content.°                                 45
Speak your griefs° softly. I do know you well.
Before the eyes of both our armies here
(Which should perceive nothing but love from us)
Let us not wrangle. Bid them move away.
Then in my tent, Cassius, enlarge° your griefs,                  50
And I will give you audience.

CASSIUS.    Pindarus,
Bid our commanders lead their charges° off
A little from this ground.

---

28 **fall** let fall
28 **crests** (a horse's crest is the neck-ridge where the mane lies)
28 **jades** horses of inferior breed (with possibly a glance in "deceitful" at the other sense of jade—faithless woman)
29 **Sink** fail
30 **Sardis** capital of ancient Lydia in Asia Minor, now part of modern Turkey (Brutus and Cassius have gone into the eastern Roman empire to raise forces against Antony and Octavius)

31 **horse in general** entire cavalry
34 **gently** slowly
14-34 **A word . . . meet him** Brutus here confers privately with his officer Lucilius, Pindarus having withdrawn a few steps with Titinius
43 **sober form** reserved manner
45 **content** calm
46 **griefs** see note III ii 220
50 **enlarge** explain
53 **charges** troops

BRUTUS.   Lucilius, do you the like; and let no man        55
     Come to our tent till we have done our conference.
     Let Lucius and Titinius guard our door.       *Exeunt.*

                ❧∼❀∼❀∼❧

        *Mane[n]t Brutus and Cassius.*         IV iii

CASSIUS.   That you have wronged me doth appear in this:
     You have condemned and noted° Lucius Pella
     For taking bribes here of the Sardians;
     Wherein my letters,° praying on his side
     Because I knew the man, was slighted off.°         5

BRUTUS.   You wronged yourself to write in such a case.

CASSIUS.   In such a time as this it is not meet
     That every nice° offense should bear his comment.°

BRUTUS.   Let me tell you, Cassius, you yourself
     Are much condemned to have° an itching palm,       10
     To sell and mart° your offices for gold
     To undeservers.

CASSIUS.   I an itching palm?
     You know that you are Brutus that speaks this,
     Or, by the gods, this speech were else your last!      15

BRUTUS.   The name of Cassius honors° this corruption,
     And chastisement doth therefore hide his head.°

CASSIUS.   Chastisement?

BRUTUS.   Remember March; the ides of March remember.
     Did not great Julius bleed for justice sake?        20
     What villain touched his body that did stab
     And not° for justice? What, shall one of us,
     That struck the foremost man of all this world

---

IV iii 2 **noted** disgraced
**4 letters** literally, the letters of which a
written message is formed, hence singular
in meaning
**5 slighted off** unheeded
**8 nice** trivial
**8 bear his comment** receive its notice

**10 condemned to have** accused of having
**11 mart** market
**16 honors** gives an appearance of honesty
to
**17 chastisement . . . head** i.e. punishment
is too embarrassed to take effect
**22 And not** except

But for supporting robbers°—shall we now
Contaminate our fingers with base bribes,                          25
And sell the mighty space of our large honors°
For so much trash as may be graspèd thus?°
I had rather be a dog and bay the moon
Than such a Roman.

CASSIUS.  Brutus, bait° not me!                                    30
I'll not endure it. You forget yourself
To hedge° me in. I am a soldier, I,
Older in practice, abler than yourself
To make conditions.°

BRUTUS.  Go to!° You are not, Cassius.                             35

CASSIUS.  I am.

BRUTUS.  I say you are not.

CASSIUS.  Urge me no more! I shall forget myself.
Have mind upon your health.° Tempt me no farther.

BRUTUS.  Away, slight° man!                                        40

CASSIUS.  Is't possible?

BRUTUS.  Hear me, for I will speak.
Must I give way and room to your rash choler?°
Shall I be frighted when a madman stares?

CASSIUS.  O ye gods, ye gods! Must I endure all this?             45

BRUTUS.  All this? Ay, more! Fret° till your proud heart break.
Go show your slaves how choleric you are
And make your bondmen tremble. Must I budge?°
Must I observe° you? Must I stand and crouch
Under your testy humor?° By the gods,                              50
You shall digest° the venom of your spleen,°

---

24 **But . . . robbers** merely for backing
dishonest officials (a new reason for the
assassination, here taken over by Shakespeare from Plutarch's account of this
quarrel, where Brutus says they killed
Caesar not for plundering the country himself, but for protecting those who did)
26 **mighty . . . honors** i.e. our power of
appointing to high public offices
27 **thus** (Brutus evidently makes a contemptuous gesture as if clutching at money)
30 **bait** provoke (with repeated attacks
like those of dogs "baiting" a chained
animal)

32 **hedge** (1) corner (like the chained animal) (?) (2) narrow my conduct to what
you approve (?)
34 **conditions** decisions
35 **Go to** nonsense
39 **health** safety
40 **slight** worthless
43 **choler** temper
46 **Fret** chafe
48 **budge** give way
49 **observe** pay court to
50 **testy humor** irritability
51 **digest** swallow
51 **spleen** organ that was once supposed
to be the generator of morose feelings and
ill nature

Though it do split you; for from this day forth
I'll use you for my mirth,° yea, for my laughter,
When you are waspish.

CASSIUS.    Is it come to this?                                    55

BRUTUS.    You say you are a better soldier.
Let it appear so; make your vaunting° true,
And it shall please me well. For mine own part,
I shall be glad to learn of noble men.°

CASSIUS.    You wrong me every way! You wrong me, Brutus!    60
I said an elder soldier, not a better.
Did I say "better"?

BRUTUS.    If you did, I care not.

CASSIUS.    When Caesar lived he durst not thus have moved°
me.

BRUTUS.    Peace, peace! You durst not so have tempted him.    65

CASSIUS.    I durst not?

BRUTUS.    No.

CASSIUS.    What? Durst not tempt him?

BRUTUS.    For your life you durst not.

CASSIUS.    Do not presume too much upon my love.               70
I may do that I shall be sorry for.

BRUTUS.    You have done that you should be sorry for.
There is no terror, Cassius, in your threats;
For I am armed so strong in honesty
That they pass by me as the idle wind,                           75
Which I respect° not. I did send to you
For certain sums of gold, which you denied me;
For I can raise no money by vile means.
By heaven, I had rather coin my heart
And drop my blood for drachmas than to wring                     80
From the hard hands of peasants their vile trash
By any indirection.° I did send
To you for gold to pay my legions,

---

53  **mirth**  object of mirth (such as a fool
or madman)
57  **vaunting**  boasting
59  **learn . . . men**  i.e. take lessons from
men who know how to behave nobly (of
whom you have just proved you are not
one)

64  **moved**  angered
76  **respect**  notice
82  **indirection**  dishonesty

Which you denied me. Was that done like Cassius?
Should I have answered Caius Cassius so?                              85
When Marcus Brutus grows so covetous
To lock such rascal counters° from his friends,
Be ready, gods, with all your thunderbolts,
Dash him to pieces!

CASSIUS.    I denied you not.                                          90

BRUTUS.    You did.

CASSIUS.    I did not. He was but a fool that brought
My answer back. Brutus hath rived° my heart.
A friend should bear his friend's infirmities,
But Brutus makes mine greater than they are.                         95

BRUTUS.    I do not, till you practise them on me.

CASSIUS.    You love me not.

BRUTUS.    I do not like your faults.

CASSIUS.    A friendly eye could never see such faults.

BRUTUS.    A flatterer's would not, though they do appear             100
As huge as high Olympus.

CASSIUS.    Come, Antony, and young Octavius, come!
Revenge yourselves alone° on Cassius.
For Cassius is aweary of the world:
Hated by one he loves; braved° by his brother;                       105
Checked° like a bondman; all his faults observed,
Set in a notebook, learned and conned by rote°
To cast into my teeth.° O, I could weep
My spirit from mine eyes! There is my dagger,
And here my naked breast; within, a heart                            110
Dearer than Pluto's° mine, richer than gold.
If that thou be'st a Roman, take it forth.
I, that denied thee gold, will give my heart.
Strike as thou didst at Caesar; for I know,
When thou didst hate him worst, thou lovedst him better              115
Than ever thou lovedst Cassius.

---

87  **rascal counters** base coins
93  **rived** broken
103 **alone** solely
105 **braved** defied
106 **Checked** rebuked

107 **conned by rote** memorized
108 **cast . . . teeth** toss in my face
111 **Pluto** god of the underworld, whom
Shakespeare here confuses with Plutus, god
of riches

BRUTUS.    Sheathe your dagger.
 Be angry when you will; it° shall have scope.°
 Do what you will; dishonor shall be humor.°
 O Cassius, you are yokèd with a lamb                          120
 That carries anger as the flint bears fire;
 Who, much enforcèd,° shows a hasty spark,
 And straight° is cold again.

CASSIUS.    Hath Cassius lived
 To be but mirth and laughter to his Brutus              125
 When grief° and blood ill-tempered° vexeth him?

BRUTUS.    When I spoke that, I was ill-tempered too.

CASSIUS.    Do you confess so much? Give me your hand.

BRUTUS.    And my heart too.

CASSIUS.    O Brutus!                                                       130

BRUTUS.    What's the matter?

CASSIUS.    Have you not love enough to bear with me
 When that rash humor° which my mother gave me
 Makes me forgetful?

BRUTUS.    Yes, Cassius; and from henceforth,                135
 When you are over-earnest with your Brutus,
 He'll think your mother chides, and leave you so.°

 *Enter a Poet [followed by Lucilius, Titinius, and Lucius].*

POET.    Let me go in to see the generals!
 There is some grudge between 'em. 'Tis not meet
 They be alone.                                                            140

LUCILIUS.    You shall not come to them.

POET.    Nothing but death shall stay me.

CASSIUS.    How now? What's the matter?

POET.    For shame, you generals! What do you mean?
 Love and be friends, as two such men should be;          145
 For I have seen more years, I'm sure, than ye.

CASSIUS.    Ha, ha! How vildly° doth this cynic° rhyme!

---

**118  it** i.e. your anger
**118  scope** free play
**119  dishonor . . . humor** any insults with
which you dishonor me I will say are just
from your hasty temper
**122  much enforcèd** forcibly struck
**123  straight** immediately

**126  grief** i.e. grievances
**126  blood ill-tempered** an unbalanced
mood
**133  rash humor** quick temper
**137  leave you so** let the matter rest
**147  vildly** vilely
**147  cynic** uncouth person

BRUTUS.   Get you hence, sirrah!° Saucy fellow, hence!

CASSIUS.   Bear with him, Brutus. 'Tis his fashion.

BRUTUS.   I'll know his humor when he knows his time.°          150
What should the wars do with these jigging° fools?
Companion,° hence!

CASSIUS.   Away, away, be gone!                         *Exit Poet.*

BRUTUS.   Lucilius and Titinius, bid the commanders
Prepare to lodge their companies to-night.             155

CASSIUS.   And come yourselves, and bring Messala with you
Immediately to us.          [*Exeunt Lucilius and Titinius.*]

BRUTUS.   Lucius, a bowl of wine.          [*Exit Lucius.*]

CASSIUS.   I did not think you could have been so angry.

BRUTUS.   O Cassius, I am sick of many griefs.               160

CASSIUS.   Of your philosophy° you make no use
If you give place° to accidental evils.°

BRUTUS.   No man bears sorrow better. Portia is dead.

CASSIUS.   Ha! Portia?

BRUTUS.   She is dead.                                         165

CASSIUS.   How scaped I killing° when I crossed you so?
O insupportable and touching loss!
Upon° what sickness?

BRUTUS.   Impatient of my absence,
And grief° that young Octavius with Mark Antony          170
Have made themselves so strong; for with her death
That tidings came.° With this she fell distract,°
And (her attendants absent) swallowed fire.

CASSIUS.   And died so?

BRUTUS.   Even so.                                            175

CASSIUS.   O ye immortal gods!

          *Enter Boy* [*Lucius*], *with wine and tapers.*

---

148 **sirrah** (cf. note III i 11)
150 **I'll . . . time** I'll accept his behavior
when he knows the right time for it
151 **jigging** rhyming
152 **Companion** (In Elizabethan speech,
often a term of contempt, as here)
161 **philosophy** i.e. as a Stoic
162 **give place** harbor, indulge
162 **accidental evils** chance misfortunes
(which the true Stoic should ignore)

166 **killing** being killed
168 **Upon** as a result of
169-70 **Impatient . . . grief** i.e. suffering
from my absence and from grief
171-72 **for . . . came** (news of Portia's
death came with news of Octavius's and
Antony's strength)
172 **distract** distraught

BRUTUS.    Speak no more of her. Give me a bowl of wine.
In this I bury all unkindness,° Cassius.                *Drinks.*

CASSIUS.    My heart is thirsty for that noble pledge.
Fill, Lucius, till the wine o'erswell the cup.                          180
I cannot drink too much of Brutus' love.
                                        [*Drinks. Exit Lucius.*]

                *Enter Titinius and Messala.*

BRUTUS.    Come in, Titinius!
Welcome, good Messala.
Now sit we close about this taper here
And call in question° our necessities.                                  185

CASSIUS.    Portia, art thou gone?

BRUTUS.    No more, I pray you.
Messala, I have here receivèd letters
That young Octavius and Mark Antony
Come down upon us with a mighty power,°                               190
Bending° their expedition° toward Philippi.°

MESSALA.    Myself have letters of the selfsame tenure.°

BRUTUS.    With what addition?

MESSALA.    That by proscription and bills of outlawry°
Octavius, Antony, and Lepidus                                          195
Have put to death an hundred senators.

BRUTUS.    Therein our letters do not well agree.
Mine speak of seventy senators that died
By their proscriptions, Cicero being one.

CASSIUS.    Cicero one?                                                 200

MESSALA.    Cicero is dead,
And by that order of proscription.
[Had you your letters from your wife, my lord?

BRUTUS.    No, Messala.

MESSALA.    Nor nothing in your letters writ of her?                    205

BRUTUS.    Nothing, Messala.

---

178 **unkindness** our misunderstandings
185 **call in question** consider
190 **power** army
191 **Bending** aiming (as a bow)
191 **expedition** speed

191 **Philippi** see 220
192 **tenure** purport
194 **by . . . outlawry** i.e. by decrees of death and other acts of condemnation

MESSALA.    That methinks is strange.

BRUTUS.    Why ask you? Hear you aught of her in yours?

MESSALA.    No, my lord.

BRUTUS.    Now as you are a Roman, tell me true.                    210

MESSALA.    Then like a Roman bear the truth I tell;
For certain she is dead, and by strange manner.

BRUTUS.    Why, farewell, Portia. We must die, Messala.
With meditating that she must die once,
I have the patience to endure it now.                              215

MESSALA.    Even so great men great losses should endure.

CASSIUS.    I have as much of this in art° as you,
But yet my nature could not bear it so.]°

BRUTUS.    Well, to our work alive.° What do you think
Of marching to Philippi° presently?                                220

CASSIUS.    I do not think it good.

BRUTUS.    Your reason?

CASSIUS.    This it is:
'Tis better that the enemy seek us.
So shall he waste his means, weary his soldiers,                   225
Doing himself offense,° whilst we, lying still,
Are full of rest, defense, and nimbleness.

BRUTUS.    Good reasons must of force° give place to better.
The people 'twixt Philippi and this ground

---

**217 in art** i.e. in my philosophical principles
**203-18 [Had you . . . so]** most editors agree that these lines represent Shakespeare's first version of Brutus's stoically self-disciplined response to Portia's death and that when he interpolated the revised version (160-77, 187), he intended the passage to be cancelled, but failed to make the intention clear on his manuscript, with the consequence that the Folio printer retained both. Efforts are sometimes made to demonstrate that no error is involved, the manifest contradictions of the two passages serving as Shakespeare's way of holding Brutus up to scorn; but the evidence for this view is not persuasive. If both passages remain, we must suppose (1) that Brutus tells Messala an outright lie in assuring him that he has heard nothing about Portia and makes a mockery of his supposed stoical self-discipline by pretending to be undergoing the shock of hearing the news for the first time, when in fact he has heard it

all before; (2) that he performs both these actions in front of a Cassius who tacitly connives at his fraud despite the high moral tone Brutus has earlier taken with respect to *his* frailties; and (3) that he manifests here a degree of hypocrisy, pettiness, and general ignobility that everything else in the play contradicts, for though often foolish and naive, he is nowhere else ignoble. Finally, we must suppose in Shakespeare an unreasonable and quite uncharacteristic expectation that a theater audience will draw all the correct inferences from this situation without being given the slightest overt clue as to what they are
**219 work alive** the tasks that as living men we face
**220 Philippi** (pronounced Philíppi) a city in Macedonia (much further from Sardis, however, than Shakespeare's conception of "marching" there "presently" allows for)
**226 offense** injury
**228 force** necessity

Do stand but in a forced affection;°                                    230
For they have grudged us contribution.°
The enemy, marching along by them,
By them shall make a fuller number up,°
Come on refreshed, new added,° and encouraged;
From which advantage shall we cut him off                               235
If at Philippi we do face him there,
These people at our back.

CASSIUS.    Hear me, good brother.

BRUTUS.    Under your pardon.° You must note beside
That we have tried the utmost° of our friends,                          240
Our legions are brimful, our cause is ripe.
The enemy increaseth every day;
We, at the height, are ready to decline.
There is a tide in the affairs of men
Which, taken at the flood, leads on to fortune;                         245
Omitted,° all the voyage of their life
Is bound in° shallows and in miseries.
On such a full sea are we now afloat,
And we must take the current when it serves
Or lose our ventures.°                                                  250

CASSIUS.    Then, with your will,° go on.
We'll along ourselves and meet them at Philippi.

BRUTUS.    The deep of night is crept upon our talk
And nature must obey necessity,
Which we will niggard with a little rest.°                              255
There is no more to say?

CASSIUS.    No more. Good night.
Early to-morrow will we rise and hence.

BRUTUS.    Lucius! (*Enter Lucius.*) My gown.°      [*Exit Lucius.*]
Farewell, good Messala.

---

**230  Do . . . affection**  support us only by
compulsion
**231  contribution**  i.e. of money and sup-
plies
**233  make . . . up**  increase its army (through
sympathizers)
**234  new added**  reinforced
**239  Under . . . pardon**  i.e. pardon me, I'm
not finished yet
**240  tried . . . utmost**  gathered all the help
we can

**246  Omitted**  not taken
**247  bound in**  confined to
**250  ventures**  all that we are venturing,
risking, in this enterprise
**251  with your will**  as you will (Cassius
lets himself be overruled, as at II i 119ff,
146ff, 162ff, and III i 21ff)
**255  Which . . . rest**  i.e. we will keep our
need for sleep to a minimum
**259  gown**  dressing gown

Good night, Titinius. Noble, noble Cassius,　　　260
Good night and good repose.

CASSIUS.　O my dear brother,
This was an ill beginning of the night!
Never come such division 'tween our souls!
Let it not, Brutus.　　　265

*Enter Lucius, with the gown.*

BRUTUS.　Everything is well.

CASSIUS.　Good night, my lord.

BRUTUS.　Good night, good brother.

TITINIUS, MESSALA.　Good night, Lord Brutus.

BRUTUS.　Farewell every one.　　　270

*Exeunt [Cassius, Titinius, and Messala].*
Give me the gown. Where is thy instrument?°

LUCIUS.　Here in the tent.

BRUTUS.　What, thou speak'st drowsily?
Poor knave,° I blame thee not; thou art o'erwatched.°
Call Claudius and some other of my men;　　　275
I'll have them sleep on cushions in my tent.

LUCIUS.　Varro and Claudius!

*Enter Varro and Claudius.*

VARRO.　Calls my lord?

BRUTUS.　I pray you, sirs, lie in my tent and sleep.
It may be I shall raise° you by and by　　　280
On business to my brother Cassius.

VARRO.　So please you, we will stand and watch your pleasure.°

BRUTUS.　I will not have it so. Lie down, good sirs.
It may be I shall otherwise bethink me.°

*[Varro and Claudius lie down.]*
Look, Lucius, here's the book I sought for so;　　　285
I put it in the pocket of my gown.

LUCIUS.　I was sure your lordship did not give it me.

---

271　**instrument**　a lute (?)
274　**knave**　boy (here, affectionate)
274　**o'erwatched**　drowsy from keeping late hours
280　**raise**　rouse

282　**watch your pleasure**　keep awake to await your orders
284　**otherwise . . . me**　change my mind

BRUTUS.    Bear with me, good boy, I am much forgetful.
Canst thou hold up thy heavy eyes awhile,
And touch° thy instrument a strain° or two?                      290

LUCIUS.    Ay, my lord, an't° please you.

BRUTUS.    It does, my boy.
I trouble thee too much, but thou art willing.

LUCIUS.    It is my duty, sir.

BRUTUS.    I should not urge thy duty past thy might.            295
I know young bloods° look for a time of rest.

LUCIUS.    I have slept, my lord, already.

BRUTUS.    It was well done; and thou shalt sleep again;
I will not hold thee long. If I do live,
I will be good to thee.                                          300

          *Music, and a song.* [*Lucius falls asleep.*]
This is a sleepy tune. O murd'rous° slumber!
Layest thou thy leaden mace° upon my boy,
That plays thee music? Gentle knave, good night.
I will not do thee so much wrong to wake thee.
If thou dost nod, thou break'st thy instrument;                 305
I'll take it from thee; and, good boy, good night.
Let me see, let me see. Is not the leaf turned down
Where I left reading? Here it is, I think.          [*Sits.*]

          *Enter the Ghost of Caesar.*

How ill this taper burns!° Ha! who comes here?
I think it is the weakness of mine eyes                          310
That shapes this monstrous apparition.
It comes upon° me. Art thou any thing?
Art thou some god, some angel, or some devil,
That mak'st my blood cold and my hair to stare?°
Speak to me what thou art.                                       315

GHOST.    Thy evil spirit, Brutus.

BRUTUS.    Why com'st thou?

---

290  **touch**  play on
290  **strain**  melody
291  **an't**  if it
296  **bloods**  constitutions
301  **murd'rous**  i.e. because it strikes a
man into an appearance of death

302  **mace**  staff with which the sheriff's
officer touched those he arrested (but the
sense of mace as club is perhaps also implicit in *murd'rous* and *leaden*)
309  **How . . . burns**  the presence of a supernatural being was supposed to cause can-
dles to dim or burn blue
312  **upon**  toward
314  **stare**  stand on end

GHOST.    To tell thee thou shalt see me at Philippi.

BRUTUS.    Well; then I shall see thee again?

GHOST.    Ay, at Philippi.                                                320

BRUTUS.    Why, I will see thee at Philippi then.    [*Exit Ghost.*]
Now I have taken heart thou vanishest.
Ill spirit, I would hold more talk with thee.
Boy! Lucius! Varro! Claudius! Sirs! Awake!
Claudius!                                                                 325

LUCIUS.    The strings, my lord, are false.°

BRUTUS.    He thinks he still is at his instrument.
Lucius, awake!

LUCIUS.    My lord?

BRUTUS.    Didst thou dream, Lucius, that thou so criedst out?          330

LUCIUS.    My lord, I do not know that I did cry.

BRUTUS.    Yes, that thou didst. Didst thou see anything?

LUCIUS.    Nothing, my lord.

BRUTUS.    Sleep again, Lucius. Sirrah Claudius! [*to Varro*]
Fellow
Thou, awake!                                                             335

VARRO.    My lord?

CLAUDIUS.    My lord?

BRUTUS.    Why did you so cry out, sirs, in your sleep?

BOTH.    Did we, my lord?

BRUTUS.    Ay. Saw you anything?                                         340

VARRO.    No, my lord, I saw nothing.

CLAUDIUS.    Nor I, my lord.

BRUTUS.    Go and commend me° to my brother Cassius.
Bid him set on his pow'rs betimes before,°
And we will follow.                                                      345

BOTH.    It shall be done, my lord.                         *Exeunt.*

---

326  **false**  out of tune
343  **commend me**  take my greetings
344  **set . . . before**  start his troops off early
ahead of me

~~~~~~

*Enter Octavius, Antony, and their Army.*                    V i

OCTAVIUS.   Now, Antony, our hopes are answerèd.°
You said the enemy would not come down
But keep the hills and upper regions.
It proves not so. Their battles° are at hand;
They mean to warn° us at Philippi here,                         5
Answering before we do demand of them.°

ANTONY.   Tut! I am in their bosoms° and I know
Wherefore they do it. They could be content
To° visit other places, and come down
With fearful bravery,° thinking by this face°                  10
To fasten in our thoughts that they have courage.
But 'tis not so.

*Enter a Messenger.*

MESSENGER.   Prepare you, generals.
The enemy comes on in gallant show;
Their bloody sign° of battle is hung out,                      15
And something to be° done immediately.

ANTONY.   Octavius, lead your battle° softly° on
Upon the left hand of the even° field.

OCTAVIUS.   Upon the right hand I. Keep thou the left.

ANTONY.   Why do you cross me in this exigent?°               20

OCTAVIUS.   I do not cross you; but I will do so.°      *March.*

*Drum. Enter Brutus, Cassius, and their Army;*
*[Lucilius, Titinius, Messala, and others].*

BRUTUS.   They stand and would have parley.°

---

**V i 1 answerèd** fulfilled
**4 battles** forces
**5 warn** challenge
**6 Answering . . . of them** retaliating before we have attacked
**7 in their bosoms** familiar with their
plans (through spies)
**8-9 could . . . To** would rather
**10 fearful bravery** (1) bravery to cover
their fear (?) (2) bravery (bravado) to inspire fear in us (?)
**10 face** show

**15 bloody sign** red flag
**16 to be** must be
**17 battle** army
**17 softly** slowly
**18 even** (1) level (?) (2) equably divided
battle array (?)
**20 exigent** crisis
**21 I . . . so** i.e. I don't do it to be defiant
or perverse, but I intend to do it all the
same
**22 parley** talk (from French *parler*)

CASSIUS.    Stand fast, Titinius. We must out and talk.

OCTAVIUS.    Mark Antony, shall we give sign of battle?

ANTONY.    No, Caesar, we will answer on their charge.°        25
Make forth.° The generals would have some words.

OCTAVIUS.    Stir not until the signal.

BRUTUS.    Words before blows. Is it so, countrymen?

OCTAVIUS.    Not that we love words better, as you do.

BRUTUS.    Good words are better than bad strokes,° Octavius.        30

ANTONY.    In your bad strokes, Brutus, you give good words;
Witness the hole you made in Caesar's heart,
Crying "Long live! Hail, Caesar!"

CASSIUS.    Antony,
The posture° of your blows are yet unknown;        35
But for your words, they rob the Hybla bees,°
And leave them honeyless.

ANTONY.    Not stingless too?°

BRUTUS.    O yes, and soundless too!
For you have stol'n their buzzing, Antony,        40
And very wisely threat before you sting.

ANTONY.    Villains! you did not so° when your vile daggers
Hacked one another in the sides of Caesar.
You showed your teeth° like apes, and fawned like hounds,
And bowed like bondmen, kissing Caesar's feet;        45
Whilst damnèd Casca, like a cur, behind
Struck Caesar on the neck.° O you flatterers!

---

25    **on their charge** when they attack
26    **Make forth** move forward
30    **bad strokes** probably general in meaning, but conceivably it contains a sarcastic glance at the many senators executed (IV iii 194-202) (?)
35    **posture** quality
36    **rob . . . bees** i.e. are so eloquently sweet that they must be honey stolen from the bees of Hybla (who were famed for the sweetness of the honey they made from the flowers growing on the slopes of Mt. Hybla in Sicily). Cassius's language may glance at Antony's eloquence in tricking the conspirators into letting him speak and in transforming the audience of citizens into a raging mob

38    **Not . . . too** (Antony's reply may refer either to his further success in rendering the conspirators "stingless," or, more probably, to the fact that his present armed power shows he has appropriated the bees' stings as well as their honey)
42    **so** i.e. buzz to show you meant to sting
44    **showed your teeth** smiled
46-47    **Casca . . . neck** Antony has had time by now to have details of the assassination from witnesses—but see III ii 181-83

CASSIUS.    Flatterers? Now, Brutus, thank yourself!
          This tongue had not offended so to-day
          If Cassius might have ruled.°                                    50

OCTAVIUS.    Come, come, the cause!° If arguing make us sweat,
          The proof° of it will turn to redder drops.
          Look, I draw a sword against conspirators.°
          When think you that the sword goes up° again?
          Never, till Caesar's three-and-thirty wounds              55
          Be well avenged, or till another Caesar°
          Have added slaughter to° the sword of traitors.

BRUTUS.    Caesar, thou canst not die by traitors' hands
          Unless thou bring'st them with thee.

OCTAVIUS.    So I hope.                                               60
          I was not born to die on Brutus' sword.

BRUTUS.    O, if thou wert the noblest of thy strain,°
          Young man, thou couldst not die more honorable.

CASSIUS.    A peevish° schoolboy,° worthless° of such honor,
          Joined with a masker and a reveller!°                       65

ANTONY.    Old Cassius still.

OCTAVIUS.    Come, Antony. Away!
          Defiance, traitors, hurl we in your teeth.
          If you dare fight to-day, come to the field;
          If not, when you have stomachs.°                            70

                    *Exit Octavius, [with] Antony, and Army.*

CASSIUS.    Why, now blow wind, swell billow,
          And swim bark!°
          The storm is up, and all is on the hazard.°

BRUTUS.    Ho, Lucilius! Hark, a word with you.

                                        *Lucilius stands forth.*

LUCILIUS.    My lord?        [*Brutus and Lucilius converse apart.*]  75

CASSIUS.    Messala.                        *Messala stands forth.*

---

50  **ruled**  had his way (see II i 162-68)
51  **the cause**  i.e. let's get to the business
52  **proof**  i.e. proving our words in action
53  **Look . . . conspirators**  (some editors divide this Folio line into two lines with breaks after "Look/conspirators")
54  **up**  back into the sheath
56  **another Caesar**  i.e. Octavius himself, Julius Caesar's nephew
57  **Have . . . to**  has met his death from

62  **strain**  line, family
64  **peevish**  (1) silly (?)  (2) ill-tempered (?)
64  **schoolboy**  (Octavius was only 21)
64  **worthless**  undeserving
65  **masker . . . reveller**  (see II ii 197 and II ii 123)
70  **stomachs**  inclination
72  **bark**  ship (Cassius views the situation in terms of a stormy sea)
73  **on the hazard**  at stake

MESSALA.   What says my general?

CASSIUS.   Messala, this is my birthday; as this° very day
  Was Cassius born. Give me thy hand, Messala.
  Be thou my witness that against my will                    80
  (As Pompey was)° am I compelled to set°
  Upon one battle all our liberties.
  You know that I held Epicurus strong
  And his opinion.° Now I change my mind
  And partly credit things that do presage.°                  85
  Coming from Sardis, on our former ensign°
  Two mighty eagles° fell;° and there they perched,
  Gorging and feeding from our soldiers' hands,
  Who to Philippi here consorted° us.
  This morning are they fled away and gone,                   90
  And in their steads do ravens, crows, and kites°
  Fly o'er our heads and downward look on us
  As we were sickly° prey. Their shadows seem
  A canopy° most fatal,° under which
  Our army lies, ready to give up the ghost.                  95

MESSALA.   Believe not so.

CASSIUS.   I but believe it partly;
  For I am fresh of spirit and resolved
  To meet all perils very constantly.°

BRUTUS.   Even so, Lucilius.°                                        100

CASSIUS.   Now, most noble Brutus,
  The gods° to-day stand friendly, that we may,
  Lovers° in peace, lead on our days to age!
  But since the affairs of men rests still° incertain,

---

**78  as this** i.e. this (Some editors combine 76, 77, and the word "Messala" of 78 into one line; 78 then begins with "This")
**81  As . . . was** (Pompey fought Caesar against his better judgment at Pharsalia and was defeated)
**81  set** (a gambling term) i.e. bet
**83-84  held . . . opinion** favored the philosophy of Epicurus (which rejected all omens as superstition on the ground that the gods were indifferent to the affairs of men)
**85  presage** predict
**86  former ensign** forward banner (as distinguished from that in the rear)
**87  eagles** birds of good omen (the birds of Jove)
**87  fell** swooped

**89  consorted** accompanied
**91  ravens . . . kites** birds of bad omen whose presence was presumed to foretell death
**93  sickly** dying
**94  canopy** bed-canopy (Cassius here speaks of the army as though it were a dying man in bed)
**94  fatal** foreboding death
**99  constantly** resolutely
**100  Even so, Lucilius** (while Cassius talks with Messala, Brutus has been talking apart with Lucilius in a conversation which these words conclude)
**102  The gods** may the gods
**103  Lovers** devoted friends
**104  rests still** remain always

Let's reason with° the worst that may befall.                    105
If we do lose this battle, then is this
The very last time we shall speak together.
What are you then determinèd to do?

BRUTUS.    Even by the rule of that philosophy°
By which I did blame Cato° for the death                    110
Which he did give himself—I know not how,
But I do find it cowardly and vile,
For fear of what might fall,° so to prevent°
The time° of life—arming myself with patience
To stay° the providence of° some high powers                    115
That govern us below.

CASSIUS.    Then, if we lose this battle,
You are contented to be led in triumph°
Thorough the streets of Rome.

BRUTUS.    No, Cassius, no.                    120
Think not, thou noble Roman,
That ever Brutus will go bound to Rome.
He bears too great a mind.° But this same day
Must end that work the ides of March begun,
And whether we shall meet again I know not.                    125
Therefore our everlasting farewell take.
For ever and for ever farewell, Cassius!
If we do meet again, why, we shall smile;
If not, why then this parting was well made.

CASSIUS.    For ever and for ever farewell, Brutus!                    130
If we do meet again, we'll smile indeed;
If not, 'tis true this parting was well made.

BRUTUS.    Why then, lead on. O that a man might know
The end of this day's business ere it come!
But it sufficeth that the day will end,                    135
And then the end is known. Come, ho! Away!        *Exeunt.*

---

**105  reason with**  consider
**109  that philosophy**  i.e. Stoicism (a main
clause such as "I shall conduct myself" is
understood before "Even")
**110  Cato**  see note II i 308
**113  fall**  befall
**113  prevent**  forestall
**114  tIme**  i.e. normal term

**115  stay**  await
**115  providence of**  destiny intended for
me by
**118  in triumph**  as a captive
**121-23  Think . . . mind**  (Brutus acknowledges that if he is captured, his "philosophy" and his actions will conflict)

❦∿❧∿❦∿❧

*Alarum.° Enter Brutus and Messala.*                 **V ii**

BRUTUS.   Ride, ride, Messala, ride, and give these bills°
    Unto the legions on the other side.°           *Loud alarum.*
    Let them set on at once; for I perceive
    But cold demeanor° in Octavius' wing,
    And sudden push gives them the overthrow.°        5
    Ride, ride, Messala! Let them all come down.°   *Exeunt.*

❦∿❧∿❦∿❧

*Alarums. Enter Cassius and Titinius.*               **V iii**

CASSIUS.   O, look, Titinius, look! The villains° fly!
    Myself° have to mine own turned enemy:
    This ensign° here of mine was turning back;
    I slew the coward and did take it° from him.

TITINIUS.   O Cassius, Brutus gave the word too early,   5
    Who, having some advantage on Octavius,
    Took it° too eagerly. His soldiers fell to spoil,°
    Whilst we by Antony are all enclosed.

*Enter Pindarus.*

PINDARUS.   Fly further off, my lord! fly further off!
    Mark Antony is in your tents, my lord.           10
    Fly, therefore, noble Cassius, fly far off!

CASSIUS.   This hill is far enough. Look, look, Titinius!
    Are those my tents where I perceive the fire?

TITINIUS.   They are, my lord.

---

**V ii s.d.   Alarum** call to arms by drums or
trumpets
**1   bills** orders
**2   side** wing of the army
**4   cold demeanor** lack of zeal
**5   gives . . . overthrow** will overthrow
them (i.e. "Octavius' wing")
**6   come down** i.e. come down from the
hills to attack

**V iii 1   villains** i.e. his own men
**2   Myself** (apparently this refers to his own
particular followers as distinguished from
the larger body of legions under his command, "mine own")
**3   ensign** standard-bearer
**4   it** i.e. the ensign's flag
**7   it** i.e. the advantage
**7   spoil** looting

CASSIUS.   Titinius, if thou lovest me,                                15
    Mount thou my horse and hide thy spurs in him°
    Till he have brought thee up to yonder troops
    And here again, that I may rest assured
    Whether yond troops are friend or enemy.

TITINIUS.   I will be here again even with a thought.°      *Exit.* 20

CASSIUS.   Go, Pindarus, get higher on that hill.
    My sight was ever thick.° Regard Titinius,
    And tell me what thou not'st about the field.
                          [*Pindarus goes up.*]
    This day I breathèd first. Time is come round,
    And where I did begin, there shall I end.                      25
    My life is run his compass.° Sirrah, what news?

PINDARUS.   (*above*°) O my lord!

CASSIUS.   What news?

PINDARUS.   [*above*] Titinius is enclosèd round about
    With horsemen that make to him on the spur.°                   30
    Yet he spurs on. Now they are almost on him.
    Now, Titinius!° Now some light.° O, he lights too!
    He's ta'en. (*Shout.*) And hark! They shout for joy.

CASSIUS.   Come down; behold no more.
    O coward that I am to live so long                              35
    To see my best friend ta'en before my face!

            *Enter Pindarus* [*from above*].

    Come hither, sirrah. In Parthas did I take thee prisoner;°
    And then I swore thee, saving of° thy life,
    That whatsoever I did bid thee do,
    Thou shouldst attempt it. Come now, keep thine oath.           40
    Now be a freeman, and with this good sword,
    That ran through Caesar's bowels, search° this bosom.
    Stand° not to answer. Here, take thou the hilts;

---

**16 hide . . . him** i.e. make him run fast
by rowelling him deeply with the spur
**20 even . . . thought** quick as a thought
**22 thick** poor
**26 compass** circuit
**27 above** i.e. on the upper stage
**30 make . . . spur** advance on him swiftly
**32 Now, Titinius!** (Pindarus speaks with
excitement, as if urging Titinius on to greater effort)

**32 light** dismount
**37 Come . . . prisoner** (divided by some
editors into two lines with breaks after
"sirrah/prisoner")
**38 swore . . . of** made you swear when
I spared your life
**42 search** penetrate
**43 Stand** wait

And when my face is covered, as 'tis now,
Guide thou the sword. [*Pindarus stabs him.*] Caesar, thou
   art revenged                                                    45
Even with the sword that killed thee.        [*Dies.*]

PINDARUS.   So, I am free;
Yet would not so° have been,
Durst I have done my will.° O Cassius!
Far from this country Pindarus shall run,                         50
Where never Roman shall take note of him.      [*Exit.*]

*Enter Titinius and Messala.*

MESSALA.   It is but change,° Titinius; for Octavius
Is overthrown by noble Brutus' power,
As Cassius' legions are by Antony.

TITINIUS.   These tidings will well comfort Cassius.              55

MESSALA.   Where did you leave him?

TITINIUS.   All disconsolate,
With Pindarus his bondman, on this hill.

MESSALA.   Is not that he that lies upon the ground?

TITINIUS.   He lies not like the living. O my heart!             60

MESSALA.   Is not that he?

TITINIUS.   No, this was he, Messala,
But Cassius is no more. O setting sun,°
As in thy red rays thou dost sink to-night,
So in his red blood Cassius' day is set!                         65
The sun of Rome is set. Our day is gone;
Clouds, dews, and dangers° come; our deeds are done!
Mistrust of my success hath done this deed.

MESSALA.   Mistrust of good success hath done this deed.
O hateful Error, Melancholy's° child,                            70
Why dost thou show to the apt° thoughts of men
The things that are not? O Error, soon conceived,

---

**48   not so**  not in this way
**49   my will**  i.e. instead of obeying Cassius
**52   change**  i.e. fair exchange
**63   setting sun**  Titinius need not be taken
to imply that it is now sunset (see 115-16),
only that the sun is now in its setting,
rather than its rising, phase and will in due
course sink with red rays into night, as
Cassius, ''The sun of Rome,'' sinks in his
red blood to death

**67   Clouds . . . dangers**  i.e. all the perils
of night (see note II i 277)
**70   Melancholy**  (which encourages errone-
ous fears)
**71   apt**  susceptible

Thou never com'st unto a happy birth,
But kill'st the mother° that engend'red thee!

TITINIUS.   What, Pindarus! Where are thou, Pindarus?                          75

MESSALA.   Seek him, Titinius, whilst I go to meet
The noble Brutus, thrusting this report
Into his ears. I may say "thrusting" it;
For piercing steel and darts envenomèd
Shall be as welcome to the ears of Brutus                                     80
As tidings of this sight.

TITINIUS.   Hie° you, Messala,
And I will seek for Pindarus the while.        [*Exit Messala.*]
Why didst thou send me forth, brave Cassius?
Did I not meet thy friends, and did not they                                  85
Put on my brows this wreath of victory,
And bid me give it thee? Didst thou not hear their shouts?
Alas, thou hast misconstrued° everything!
But hold thee,° take this garland on thy brow.
Thy Brutus bid me give it thee, and I                                         90
Will do his bidding. Brutus, come apace°
And see how I regarded Caius Cassius.
By your leave, gods. This is a Roman's part.°
Come, Cassius' sword, and find Titinius' heart.               *Dies.*

          *Alarum. Enter Brutus, Messala, Young Cato,*
               *Strato, Volumnius, and Lucilius.*

BRUTUS.   Where, where, Messala, doth his body lie?                            95

MESSALA.   Lo, yonder, and Titinius mourning it.

BRUTUS.   Titinius' face is upward.

CATO.   He is slain.

BRUTUS.   O Julius Caesar, thou art mighty yet!
Thy spirit walks abroad and turns our swords                                  100
In our own proper° entrails.                          *Low alarums.*

CATO.   Brave Titinius!
Look whe'r he have not° crowned dead Cassius.

---

74 **mother** i.e. the melancholy person (in
this case, Cassius) who conceived and gave
birth to the error
82 **Hie** hurry
88 **misconstrued** (pronounced miscón-
stered)

89 **hold thee** wait a moment
91 **apace** quickly
93 **part** proper role
101 **own proper** very own
103 **Look . . . not** i.e. Look how he has

BRUTUS.   Are yet two Romans living such as these?
　　　The last of all the Romans,° fare thee well!                    105
　　　It is impossible that ever Rome
　　　Should breed thy fellow.° Friends, I owe moe° tears
　　　To this dead man than you shall see me pay.
　　　I shall find time, Cassius; I shall find time.
　　　Come therefore, and to Thasos° send his body.               110
　　　His funerals shall not be in our camp,
　　　Lest it discomfort us.° Lucilius, come;
　　　And come, young Cato. Let us to the field.
　　　Labeo and Flavius set° our battles° on.
　　　'Tis three o'clock; and, Romans, yet ere night             115
　　　We shall try fortune in a second fight.         *Exeunt.*

　　　*Alarum. Enter Brutus, Messala, [Young] Cato,*          V iv
　　　　　*Lucilius, and Flavius.*

BRUTUS.   Yet, countrymen, O, yet hold up your heads!
　　　　　*[Exit, followed by Messala and Flavius.]*

CATO.   What bastard° doth not? Who will go with me?
　　　I will proclaim my name about the field.
　　　I am the son of Marcus Cato,° ho!
　　　A foe to tyrants, and my country's friend.                   5
　　　I am the son of Marcus Cato, ho!

　　　　　*Enter Soldiers and fight.*

LUCILIUS.   And I am Brutus, Marcus Brutus I!
　　　Brutus, my country's friend! Know me for Brutus!°

---

**105 The . . . Romans** (Shakespeare has
Brutus apply to Cassius the phrase that the
Roman historian Livy applies to Cassius and
Brutus: *ultimi Romanorum*, "the last of the
(true) Romans")
**107 fellow** equal
**107 moe** more
**110 Thasos** island near Philippi
**112 discomfort us** dishearten our forces
**114 set** are setting
**114 battles** troops
**V iv 2 What bastard** i.e. who so lacks true
Roman blood that he
**4 Marcus Cato** see note II i 308

**7-8 And I . . . Brutus** the Folio gives
these lines to Cato along with 2-6, and
gives only 9-11 to Lucilius. Since it is clear,
however, from 15 that Lucilius is imperson-
ating Brutus in order to draw the enemy
attackers to himself (as he does also in
Shakespeare's source), it seems reasonable
to suppose that the Folio speech-heading
"Lucil." was slipped down two lines by
mistake. The Folio does not have Brutus exit
after 1, but presumably should so that he
goes off to rally other troops while Lucilius
impersonates him here in the meantime

[*Young Cato falls.*]

O young and noble Cato, art thou down?
Why, now thou diest as bravely as Titinius,                    10
And mayst be honored, being Cato's son.

[1.] SOLDIER.   Yield, or thou diest.

LUCILIUS.   Only I yield° to die.
There is so much that° thou wilt kill me straight.°
Kill Brutus, and be honored in his death.                      15

[1.] SOLDIER.   We must not. A noble prisoner!

*Enter Antony.*

2. SOLDIER.   Room ho! Tell Antony Brutus is ta'en.

1. SOLDIER.   I'll tell the news. Here comes the general.
Brutus is ta'en! Brutus is ta'en, my lord!

ANTONY.   Where is he?                                          20

LUCILIUS.   Safe, Antony; Brutus is safe enough.
I dare assure thee that no enemy
Shall ever take alive the noble Brutus.
The gods defend him from so great a shame!
When you do find him, or alive or dead,                        25
He will be found like Brutus, like himself.°

ANTONY.   This is not Brutus, friend; but, I assure you,
A prize no less in worth. Keep this man safe;
Give him all kindness. I had rather have
Such men my friends than enemies. Go on,                       30
And see whe'r Brutus be alive or dead;
And bring us word unto Octavius' tent
How every thing is chanced.°                        *Exeunt.*

---

**13 Only I yield** I yield only that I may
**14 There . . . that** (1) there is so much
reason for you to kill me, since I am
Brutus, that (?) (2) there [offering gold] is
a sum that is yours if (?)

**14 straight** immediately
**26 like himself** true to his nature
**33 is chanced** has turned out

*Enter Brutus, Dardanius, Clitus, Strato, and Volumnius.*          V v

BRUTUS.    Come, poor remains° of friends, rest on this rock.

CLITUS.    Statilius showed the torchlight;° but, my lord,
He came not back. He is or ta'en or slain.

BRUTUS.    Sit thee down, Clitus. Slaying is the word.
It is a deed in fashion. Hark thee, Clitus.          [*Whispers.*] 5

CLITUS.    What, I, my lord? No, not for all the world!

BRUTUS.    Peace then. No words.

CLITUS.    I'll rather kill myself.

BRUTUS.    Hark thee, Dardanius.                    [*Whispers.*]

DARDANIUS.    Shall I do such a deed?                          10

CLITUS.    O Dardanius!

DARDANIUS.    O Clitus!

CLITUS.    What ill request did Brutus make to thee?

DARDANIUS.    To kill him, Clitus. Look, he meditates.

CLITUS.    Now is that noble vessel full of grief,          15
That° it runs over even at his eyes.

BRUTUS.    Come hither, good Volumnius. List° a word.

VOLUMNIUS.    What says my lord?

BRUTUS.    Why this, Volumnius.
The ghost of Caesar hath appeared to me          20
Two several° times by night—at Sardis once,
And this last night here in Philippi fields.
I know my hour is come.

VOLUMNIUS.    Not so, my lord.

BRUTUS.    Nay, I am sure it is, Volumnius.          25
Thou seest the world, Volumnius, how it goes.
Our enemies have beat us to the pit.°          *Low alarums.*
It is more worthy to leap in ourselves
Than tarry till they push us. Good Volumnius,
Thou know'st that we two went to school together.          30

---

V v 1 **poor remains** wretched survivors
**2 showed the torchlight** flashed a signal
from the enemy camp
**16 That** so that
**17 List** hear

**21 several** separate
**27 beat . . . pit** driven us to the pitfall (for
trapping animals)

Even for that our love of old, I prithee
Hold thou my sword-hilts whilst I run on it.

CLITUS.     Fly, fly, my lord! There is no tarrying here.

VOLUMNIUS.     That's not an office for a friend, my lord.

*Alarum still.*°

BRUTUS.     Farewell to you; and you; and you, Volumnius.     35
Strato, thou hast been all this while asleep.
Farewell to thee too, Strato. Countrymen,
My heart doth joy that yet in all my life
I found no man but he was true to me.
I shall have glory by this losing day     40
More than Octavius and Mark Antony
By this vile° conquest shall attain unto
So fare you well at once;° for Brutus' tongue
Hath almost ended his life's history.
Night hangs upon mine eyes; my bones would rest,     45
That have but labored to attain this hour.°

*Alarum. Cry within:* Fly, fly, fly!

CLITUS.     Fly, my lord, fly!

BRUTUS.     Hence! I will follow.

*[Exeunt Clitus, Dardanius, and Volumnius.]*
I prithee, Strato, stay thou by thy lord.     50
Thou art a fellow of a good respect;°
Thy life hath had some smatch° of honor in it.
Hold then my sword, and turn away thy face
While I do run upon it. Wilt thou, Strato?

STRATO.     Give me your hand first. Fare you well, my lord.     55

BRUTUS.     Farewell, good Strato. Caesar, now be still.
I killed not thee with half so good a will.

*[He runs on his sword and] dies.*

*Alarum. Retreat. Enter Octavius, Antony,*
*Messala, Lucilius, and the Army.*

---

**34 s.d. still** continuing
**42 vile** i.e. because it will end the Roman Republic and begin the rule of one man
**43 at once** i.e. without more delay

**46 but . . . hour** i.e. their labor has been aimed only at achieving the rest from labor that death brings (for the Stoic, a noble death was a form of fulfillment)
**51 respect** reputation
**52 smatch** smack, i.e. relish

OCTAVIUS.   What man° is that?

MESSALA.   My master's man. Strato, where is thy master?

STRATO.   Free from the bondage you are in, Messala.               60
　　　The conquerors can but make a fire of him;°
　　　For Brutus only overcame himself,°
　　　And no man else hath honor by his death.

LUCILIUS.   So Brutus should be found. I thank thee, Brutus,
　　　That thou hast proved Lucilius' saying° true.                  65

OCTAVIUS.   All that served Brutus, I will entertain° them.
　　　Fellow, wilt thou bestow thy time with me?

STRATO.   Ay, if Messala will prefer° me to you.

OCTAVIUS.   Do so, good Messala.

MESSALA.   How died my master, Strato?                              70

STRATO.   I held the sword, and he did run on it.

MESSALA.   Octavius, then take him to follow thee,
　　　That did the latest° service to my master.

ANTONY.   This° was the noblest Roman of them all.
　　　All the conspirators save only he                             75
　　　Did that they did in envy of great Caesar;
　　　He, only in a general honest thought°
　　　And common good to all, made one of° them.
　　　His life was gentle,° and the elements°
　　　So mixed° in him that Nature might stand up                   80
　　　And say to all the world, "This was a man!"

OCTAVIUS.   According to his virtue let us use° him,
　　　With all respect and rites of burial.
　　　Within my tent his bones to-night shall lie,
　　　Most like a soldier, orderèd° honorably.                      85
　　　So call the field° to rest, and let's away
　　　To part° the glories of this happy day.        *Exeunt omnes.*

---

58  **man** servant
61  **make . . . him** burn his body
62  **Brutus . . . himself** only Brutus defeated Brutus
65  **saying** (see V iv 22-26)
66  **entertain** attach to my service
68  **prefer** recommend
73  **latest** last
74  **This** i.e. Brutus
77  **general . . . thought** i.e. public spirit

78  **made one of** joined
79  **gentle** noble
79  **elements** i.e. the four so-called humors or temperaments—melancholic, phlegmatic, sanguine, choleric
80  **mixed** balanced, well-proportioned
82  **use** treat
85  **orderèd** treated
86  **field** armies
87  **part** divide

# In the Theater of the Mind

*i*

The comments that follow are meant to suggest ways of internally *visualizing* and *feeling* the play, which are essential if the reading of it is not to be merely an intellectual exercise. Few of us get a chance to see professional productions of Shakespeare, and that's a pity; the lines well spoken, the parts well acted have a profound impact that is hard to duplicate in the study. Nevertheless, the life of a Shakespearean play *is* in the lines, and an imaginative reader can realize that life in the theater of his own mind. Shakespeare's Globe demanded of the audience a ready ear and an inward eye—a willingness to transcend what they saw before them in order to transform it imaginatively into a world that neither eye nor ear actually quite caught. A reader can do the same, and, once he has learned how, is better off in doing it for himself by the activity of his own imagination than he is in passively allowing a stage or film director to do it for him. Even the greatest of professional productions remains subject, in the end, to the image of the play's potentialities that exists in a seasoned playgoer's, or a seasoned reader's, mind.

Since we are not directly concerned here with how the play should be produced in the theater, but rather how parts of it may be realized in the imagination, we refer to actual staging only to point out what the language indicates is going on inside and outside the characters. On the same grounds, we make no attempt to "cover" the total action in any chronological way. Our observations on particular scenes are intended to suggest ways of looking at others as well.

*ii*

In *Julius Caesar,* as we remarked in the introduction, the interplay between the demands and values of private and public behavior, as embodied in the actions of two quite different sets of men, provides the moving force behind the play. One set, Brutus and Cassius, dominates the first half (roughly the first three acts of the text). The other set, Caesar (now dead), Antony, and Octavius, dominates the second half. Brutus and Cassius, the *actors* of the first half, become the *reactors* of the second, and from this change of role both the high dramatic arguments and the play's tragic import emerge.

Caesar and Antony—forces that respectively shape the actions and reactions of Brutus and Cassius—point up the basic nature of this Roman world. It is primarily a public world, one in which accomplished rhetoric is the natural dramatic language, but it is also a world in which *presence* is everything. All the major figures are accomplished speakers, but while Brutus has confidence in language primarily as a medium for ideas, Caesar and Antony know that it is the continuing presence of the speaker, and all that that presence represents, which determines action and events.

Around these figures Shakespeare has placed as a frame two strikingly different crowd scenes. The commoners of the first (I i) are individualized persons who react in sharply comic terms to the haranguing of Flavius and Marullus, while the plebeians of III iii are faceless shouters easily whipped up by Antony into a destructive mob. Between these two scenes, Brutus, Cassius, Caesar, and Antony present a world whose form is very much the result of the art of persuasion, but in these scenes involving the commoners and plebeians we get a strikingly different image of a world of unpredictable and violent change that runs against the tide in the affairs of public men.

To present these contrasting worlds in the theater, a good set might be a series of permanent and balanced platforms leading downstage to an open playing area (with a small seating elevation) extending into the audience. The platforms serve as an effective visual symbol of the clarity, stability, and directness of the Roman world, against which the fluid and ambiguous movements of men and crowds will stand out and suggest the irrational and disordered confusion to which human beings, even the most reasonable and philosophical, are prone.

*iii*

We should imagine the first scene beginning with the boisterous physical action of the commoners as they surge onstage in holiday mood bordering on drunken riot. They move freely and quickly over the platform areas and downstage so that Flavius and Marullus can make a quick upstage center entrance and move down immediately to quell the disorder. The tribunes then move to speak to individuals on various platforms during the opening dialogue (i 1-31), with Marullus finally taking the center of the stage for his major speech to the crowd, backed up immediately by Flavius. Through these major speeches the commoners fall silent and leave the stage in small groups going in various directions, the last group withering sheepishly away as Flavius finishes reprimanding them. The tribunes then speak their final lines downstage and make a quick exit as the trumpets sound for Caesar's entrance.

A sharp contrast to the noise and confusion of the first scene is provided by the entrance of Caesar and his train in the second. The entrance is a processional with everyone taking balanced positions on the platforms and downstage, surrounding Caesar at the center with Calphurnia. Everything that happens in the first twenty-eight lines is determined by Caesar from his central position, including the sounding of the three passages of music and the general movement of the crowd. This establishes such a sense of public occasion that Caesar's brief lines on Calphurnia's barrenness convey unmistakably the impression that Caesar is totally the public man, even where private matters are concerned. To strengthen that impression, contemporary theater practice often brings the soothsayer on from the audience, having Caesar look toward the audience as he attempts to identify him. At the great man's command all move upstage and out, leaving Brutus and Cassius in the downstage area for the next part of the scene.

From Cassius's opening lines the dialogue builds powerfully in three stages, interrupted by offstage flourishes and shouts which Brutus fears to be the signals of Caesar's acceptance of a crown. Brutus remains comparatively motionless at center while

Cassius slowly moves around him through his own speeches. As Brutus attempts to break from Cassius at the end of each stage of the argument, he is stopped by a flourish. His tragic inability to break from the fatal tension between private and public concerns is thus visually highlighted early in the action. After his puzzled response to the first flourish, Cassius takes the center of the stage for his long narrative on Caesar's human weaknesses (ii 100-41), while Brutus sits reflectively listening. At the second flourish, Brutus, with the startled "Another general shout?" jumps suddenly to his feet. In response, Cassius delivers his next speech (145-71) with fevered intensity and agitated movement up and down the platform areas, until Brutus finally restrains him by putting a hand on his shoulder and speaking his reply in a tone of quiet reassurance. The emotional disorder which Cassius has introduced into the scene is now recapitulated in the public context with the disordered re-entrance of Caesar and his train. Caesar himself does not come stage center again, but hovers by the side for his conversation with Antony about Cassius. In contrast to his ceremonious first appearance, the exit to the side of the stage with Antony is effectively informal and quiet as the private man suddenly looks out of the public mask:

> Come on my right hand, for this ear is deaf,
> And tell me truly what thou think'st of him. (225-26)

The play now moves through a series of sudden contrasts. Casca takes stage center with Brutus and Cassius to establish a lighter mood of rough cynicism in his description of Caesar's refusal of the crown. The use here of prose allows for a variety of tone and pace and an easy, informal movement about the stage. Casca's exit is quickly followed by Brutus's, and Cassius is left alone to create in his soliloquy the ominous atmosphere that leads into the thunder and lightning of the next scene (I iii). The storm offers a rich theatrical comparison to the fanfares and processional music that we heard only a short time ago, and provides a background which demands that the lines be spoken loudly and quickly, building a firm sense of the rapidly forming conspiracy and the final ensnaring of Brutus.

*iv*

In II i we need to comprehend fully both Brutus's inability to reconcile public obligation with private sensibility (61-69) and his deep attachment to Portia, which will lead him to reveal himself completely to her later (245-323). Since he never states directly to the conspirators why or how he has been able to resolve his doubts, it is important that in the early part of the scene he put himself close to the audience so that we may identify with his doubts and uncertainties, and that when the conspirators enter, he move far upstage with Cassius, while Decius, Casca, and Cinna move downstage for their conversation (106-16). The intervention of this conversation cuts us off momentarily from Brutus. He does not *dramatically* resolve his doubts, but returns to the center of action in a moment to direct the assassination and the special form it must take. The effect is that we get Brutus's feelings toward the conspirators and Portia, but that his thought remains hidden or at least incomplete. The case for assassination has not been fully articulated.

The sequence between Brutus and Portia should be played simply and directly for its sense of deep love and fidelity between husband and wife. Brutus, for the most part, listens quietly and intently to Portia, embracing her after his line: "O ye gods,/ Render me worthy of this noble wife!" It is a moment of quiet respite before the thunder motif returns to take us to Caesar and the tension of the conspirators' arrival at his house to escort him to the Capitol. Caesar should remain at stage center so that Calphurnia, the servant, and Decius are all placed in positions suggesting suitors appealing to an important personage. The scene thus gains a formal quality that contrasts strongly with the informality of the dialogue between Brutus and Portia just preceding. In that dialogue, Brutus turns frequently from Portia to emphasize to the audience his attempts to keep his wife uninvolved in painful affairs. Caesar, on the other hand, remains stolidly facing his listeners, attempting to impress them with his unshakable determination. Even in the privacy of his own home, he is still the public personage of I ii. He keeps the same uniform, authoritarian tone to Calphurnia on his right and Decius on his left, even though he is ironically changing under the influence of Decius's flattering interpretation of Calphurnia's dream. Since Caesar is occupying virtually the same stage area he will take in III i when he insists upon his being as "constant as the Northern Star," the memory of this moment will give particular poignancy to the final moments of his life.

The dramatic pace quickens effectively in the short sequences of II iii and iv with the staccato crispness of Artemidorus's letter and brief following speech delivered at one side of the stage, followed immediately at the other side by the highly excited entrance of Portia and Lucius. Portia should enter distraught, hair down, pushing Lucius before her. She moves downstage for her aside; he follows in confusion and amazement. When Portia thinks she hears noise from the Capitol, she rushes to the center of the stage as the soothsayer appears from the other side. He speaks his lines with perfect control, which in contrast to the high excitement of Portia's lines provides the sequence with a tone of ominous foreshadowing. His speech, ". . . if it will please Caesar/To be so good to Caesar as to hear me:/I shall beseech him to befriend himself" (32-34) brings Portia almost to the breaking point, so that her final words are delivered with a sense of exhaustion and near despair. The tragic note, central to the scenes of the assassination and Caesar's funeral, is already struck here.

*v*

Like most sequences in the action, visualizing the assassination itself is primarily a matter of following the structural implications of the lines. Caesar should, of course, use one of the elevations at stage center to emphasize both his own arrogance and the feigned servility of Metellus Cimber and Cassius as they kneel before him. As Brutus kneels, Caesar's attention is fully on him as he gives his "What, Brutus?" During this exchange Casca moves up behind Caesar while Cinna, Decius, and Cassius are ready to move in from the sides. On "Doth not Brutus bootless kneel?" Caesar moves down toward Brutus, at which point Casca suddenly stabs from behind on "Speak hands for me!" The others quickly move in, with Brutus stabbing last; then a quick break by all the assassins, and Brutus and Caesar are at stage center for "Et tu Brutè?—Then fall Caesar." If Caesar falls against Brutus, staining him with blood, and bringing him a sudden realization of horror as he stares at it, the sense of unanticipated consequence, of idea transformed into fact, that is so strong in this play will receive an effective visual emphasis. Brutus moves away slowly during the immediate reactions of Cinna and Cassius, continuing to stare at the blood on his hands and clothes, regaining composure with "People and senators, be not affrighted," and the following lines to Publius. The lines on fate (108-10) are given with philosophical resignation. He is now ready to treat the death of Caesar as ritualistic sacrifice (115-20).

When Antony enters, he quickly takes possession of stage center in the area of Caesar's body, becoming thereby a kind of living extension of Caesar's dead presence, virtually controlling the remainder of the first half of the play. He first laments the death of Caesar and then daringly challenges the conspirators to destroy him also (162-77). When the others, particularly Brutus, so quickly reassure him, he delivers his response with quiet, unnoticed irony, and moves from one conspirator to the next shaking hands, a kind of formal ritual that stands as ironic comment on the solemn ritual that Brutus and the others have just performed. When the others exit, he remains by Caesar's body to speak in a way that tells us his grief is real (274-95). The entrance of Octavius's servant provides a renewal of dramatic movement to take us down from the emotional peak of Antony's words. The servant's grief for Caesar is simple in comparison and thus enables Antony to recover from the power of his own reaction to move on with dramatic flow:

> Thy heart is big. Get thee apart and weep.
> Passion, I see, is catching; for mine eyes,
> Seeing those beads of sorrow stand in thine,
> Began to water. Is thy master coming? (302-5)

*vi*

In III ii and iii we have the major climax of the play, two scenes which can be played as an unbroken unit. It is a valid stage tradition that Brutus and Antony deliver their orations from an elevated platform upstage center. This allows the maximum amount of free stage area on both secondary platforms and main stage level for the movement of the crowd. The plebeians may be placed in a large, irregular circular pattern full across the stage. One or two close to the pulpit area may cue in other crowd responses at high points of tension simply by turning to face other plebeians and the audience. To keep the audience intensely involved, as part of the crowd in a sense, some plebeians should be placed in the front of the auditorium itself close to the forestage. Stage lighting can be of great assistance if a realistic, broad daylight effect is used in the opening part of the scene through Brutus's speech while the crowd is still responding as a group of individuals. When Antony begins to work on them, the lighting should shift gradually toward strong light and shadow contrasts, finally achieving a fully grotesque, distorted, and irrational atmosphere in the scene of the murder of Cinna. All stage effect, however, should be properly subordinated to the voices of Brutus and Antony and the responding crowd.

The funeral scene works effectively if the crowd is agitated at the beginning, pressing around Brutus and Cassius in the downstage area but quickly quieted by Brutus as he reassures them in his opening lines, which show a Brutus calmly confident of his personal incorruptibility and reputation for public concern. His integrity leads him to impute to his listeners the same response to the death of Caesar that he himself describes in his speech (14-29), and he therefore assumes that his audience must necessarily respond to his high-minded appeal for selfless patriotism. His words should be heard with a sustained tone of quiet authority and sure conviction. A stronger emotional appeal comes in the direct questions that follow (29-34) when the crowd responds with wholehearted support for Brutus. But then Antony enters with Caesar's body.

Antony might well make this entrance unobtrusively, but close to the audience, so that we are fully aware of his presence through the concluding part of Brutus's scene. When Brutus announces Antony's entrance (41), the crowd turns momentarily toward him with awe and curiosity, but they quickly turn back to Brutus as he concludes his address. They surge up to him with enthusiasm (48-55) and then move eagerly back downstage as Brutus leaves and Antony goes into the pulpit.

Antony's oration is a blend of words and actions carefully planned to capture the crowd that has shown its devotion to Brutus. By presenting his own grief with a tone of deep sincerity leading to the pause for supposed tears (80-114), he wins the emotional sympathy of the plebeians. Then Caesar's will becomes a highly effective stage prop to inflame the crowd with a new and different kind of interest (135-75) and to move Antony down center to Caesar's body for the verbal reenactment of the assassination (176-204). This totally wins the crowd so that he can finally attack the conspirators directly, send the crowd surging up and over the upstage platform, but then call them back so as to redouble their violence through the reading of the will. At his "Here was a Caesar! When comes such another?" they break quickly from him and rush out upstage to return from the same area in a few moments for the Cinna scene. The sudden calm of his "Now let it work. Mischief, thou art afoot,/Take thou what course thou wilt" will have a sinister effect as the servant enters. The servant's description of how Brutus and Cassius "Are rid like madmen through the gates of Rome" is dramatic economy at its best, leading to a quick exit by him and Antony.

Cinna enters immediately. He establishes in his opening lines an ominous mood that is suddenly broken by the entrance of the enraged plebeians, who individually surround him as they enter from upstage right and left, moving down over the platform areas to hem in the isolated figure of the poet. This downstage movement is most natural to the plebeians' lines (5-12). Since the grim comic effect of this brief scene lies partially in the highly theatrical sense of the grotesque that develops, we might well imagine the use of strong side-lighting on the actors in order to emphasize the grotesque by throwing large shadows on the upstage wall. When this effect is realized, the ensuing dialogue indicates a kind of quiet plateau on which the actors can remain comparatively motionless for a moment to play out the menacing humor of the lines.

At line 28, when Cinna gives his name and the plebeians mistake him for one of Caesar's assassins, a new and powerful effect is thrust into the scene. A change of emphasis in lighting could heighten the sudden upsurge of shouting voices and the feeling of terror that Cinna must convey as the scene sweeps to its grisly end. "Tear him for his bad verses! Tear him for his bad verses!" is dark comedy still, but grotesque in the context of the mounting hysteria of these final moments. We are thus prepared verbally for the major climax, which lies not in the words, but in the action toward which all the elements in the scene have been working. That climax is, of course, the brutal slaying of Cinna at the cry of "Tear him, tear him!" These words cue a sudden burst of physical movement from the crowd to grasp Cinna and kill him, after which we can imagine a prolonged pause as the blood lust for further violence is registered in pantomime. Then with "Come, brands, ho! . . ." the plebeians rush from the stage holding the body of Cinna on high. The first half of the play ends, then, on a note of major theatrical intensity, and the dramatic significance of Antony's oration in the previous scene is underscored.

*vii*

The new image of authority in the world is chillingly realized in IV i as Antony and Octavius plan the campaign against Brutus and Cassius with passionless detachment. The words need to be heard with only a quiet, tight-lipped firmness that carries the sense that action is now not a matter of deep, passionate involvement, but of pragmatic calculation. Perhaps the most telling detail in the scene is Antony's reference to Caesar's will, that object used to drive a crowd to absolute frenzy in the previous act. Now, in the new "action," it is merely a prop in the practical scheme of things:

> But, Lepidus, go you to Caesar's house.
> Fetch the will hither, and we shall determine
> How to cut off some charges in legacies. (8-10)

Such is the new order for which the assassination of Caesar has opened the door.

In the entrance of the armies of Brutus and Cassius, IV ii offers a good example of how the military scenes of the final act of the play can be visualized. Brutus's soldiers enter and remain on the upstage platform at the right; Cassius's soldiers make a similar entrance at the left. Brutus and Cassius come downstage for their private dialogue (40-51). At their commands the armies exit upstage, Brutus and Cassius move further downstage, and the forestage now becomes the "tent" for the intense private scene that follows.

In this scene, the major movement consists of one speaker advancing on the other with particularly strong words. The other reacts either by standing his ground if he soon has to make a strong advance of his own, or by turning away sharply, giving his opponent pointed motivation for further attack. The strong attack is illustrated by Brutus's major speech (19-29), which reveals both his greatness and his blindness, his lofty idealism and his poor judgment of the motives of his fellow conspirators. Cassius stands his ground with a passage of pure emotionalism (30-34) and Brutus turns sharply away (35). Cassius reaches an emotional peak when he offers Brutus his dagger and urges him to kill him (108-15), providing the opportunity for an interesting piece of stage business. If Cassius and Brutus are standing at this moment in virtually the same positions occupied by Caesar and Brutus in the assassination scene, then Brutus might take the extended dagger, look at it sadly for a moment, recalling the assassination, and by his silence as he hands the dagger back, render a sense of the quiet melancholy and weariness that will increasingly overwhelm him until his suicide. Such a piece of business provides the necessary transition to the more understated playing of his reconciliation with Cassius and his revelation of Portia's death.

The remainder of the scene is particularly interesting for its image of a Brutus who grows affectingly human in defeat. Such a human moment lies in the passage spoken by Brutus to the boy, Lucius, immediately before the ghost of Caesar appears (285-306). Here we see what Shakespeare, perhaps more than any other dramatist, can realize out of small particulars, the reaction of a great protagonist to the loyalty of an ordinary servant and to a passage of music. In such a moment, there is a magnificent rendering of the commonplaces of life, a marvelous opportunity for an actor to project the quietly intense drama of little things deeply felt—a man's weariness, the love of books, of music, of faithful servants—before he wheels to face the ghost of Caesar upstage. The ghost sequence is played simply for its basic elements, and we are pointed to the military action of the final act.

*viii*

The play ends with the body of Brutus in a position onstage similar to Caesar's after the assassination, with Antony and Octavius standing over it at right and left for their final speeches. The speaking of these is of special importance. Antony's words (74-81) pick up the sense of the richer values of the private world of action, the world that Brutus makes us so poignantly aware of in these final scenes. The lines should be said with a tone of rich, personal warmth. Octavius, on the other hand, delivers his speech (82-87) in the manner of public oratory; the tone is one of formal tribute giving way to the harder practicality of the final lines:

> So call the field to rest, and let's away
> To part the glories of this happy day.

For most of its span of action, then, the play burns with the hard, clear light of public affairs. This is an action we have stressed in our commentary through the visualizing of many sequences on upstage platforms. But in the more private scenes, played slowly and reflectively in the downstage areas, we have received intimations of the futility of rule; of the apparent impossibility of sustaining order for very long in man's world or in a man himself; of the darker presence of storm, portent, the irrational, the heavy weight of melancholy weariness. In these scenes we move closer and closer to the heart of darkness that is tragedy.

# STUDY QUESTIONS

## ESSAY QUESTIONS

1. Take as your lead any of the following comments on *Julius Caesar* and write a paper developing the idea, or qualifying it, or refuting it—or a combination of all three:

   (a) "What . . . of the great shadow of Caesar which looms over the whole? Let us admit that, even while he lives and speaks, it is more shadow than substance. Is it too harsh a comment that Caesar is in the play merely to be assassinated?"

   (b) "Unless Caesar is seen as more than a person in this play, then his name should never have been given to a tragedy in which he appears, unghosted, in only three scenes, and speaks in a mere hundred and fifty lines. His body lies in full view of the stage during two scenes, each of which is considerably longer than the sum of the lines Caesar speaks in the entire play. Stage pictures and silence may point a moral."

   (c) "Between . . . Brutus and . . . Antony a plain issue is set. It is righteousness matched against efficiency and showing itself clearly impotent in the unequal contest. Had we only to do with the fate of individuals, it might pass. But the selection of the artist makes his puppets more than individuals. They stand for spiritual forces, and in the spiritual order the triumph of efficiency over righteousness is tragic stuff."

   (d) "*Julius Caesar* is more rhetoric than poetry, just as its persons are more orators than men. They all have something of the statue in them, for they express their author's idea of antiquity rather than his knowledge of life."

(e)        " 'There is no terror, Cassius, in your threats,
           For I am armed so strong in honesty [integrity]
           That they pass by me as the idle wind,
           Which I respect [heed] not.'

It is the perfect echo of an earlier speech in the play. The arrogation of moral infallibility is but a step below the affectation of divinity. Brutus has become like Caesar! His victim has infected him with his own disease. It is the special nemesis of the revolutionist. He comes to resemble what he once abhorred."

(f) "On a first reading of the play, we wonder why Shakespeare did not call it *Brutus;* on a second reading, we understand."

2. How central to the play is the *killing* of Caesar? If the conspirators had simply overthrown him and exiled him, in what ways would the present Act II have to be revised? What other scenes would be affected, and why? Write a paper discussing these questions, or, alternatively, write a prose version of the speeches that you imagine Brutus and Antony would have made if Caesar's fate had been exile.

3. Consider in a paper or in a modified promptbook how III i might be managed on an ordinary school or college stage with a limited number of actors and props. How would you achieve the mob effect? How would you select what the audience shall see and hear, by arrangement of the stage? How would you dress Brutus and Antony so as to suit their roles here? How would you handle the killing, and Caesar's body after it?

QUESTIONS

[*I i*]

1. What purposes are served by the first scene? (You will be helped in answering this question if you (a) compare the actual opening of the play with other possible openings, e.g. a scene like I ii or II i; and (b) consider the following subquestions carefully.)

(a) How much background information is given? Make a list of the pieces of information the scene provides about each of the following: (1) Caesar, (2) the populace as a whole, (3) their elected representatives (the tribunes Flavius and Marullus).

(b) Why all the smart-aleck punning by the cobbler at the beginning? What does it reveal about the crowd's initial attitude toward the tribunes? How does its attitude change later on in the scene? The plebeians have a very important mass role in the play. Jot down three or four points that you would want to make about their behavior and attitude as revealed in the first scene if you were assigned a paper on the subject. Later, you should consider whether the same characteristics persist in future scenes.

(c) What are the tribunes' objections to the crowd's holiday spirit? Are they simply sour souls who can't stomach people having a good time? Or self-important little big shots who envy Caesar his popularity and power? What is Caesar returning in power from? How does their attitude throw light on the conflict that we see developing in I ii and I iii? What is the expression of that conflict in this scene?

(d) Who do you suppose has "decked" the statues of Caesar "with ceremonies" (line 66)? Why? Do you think the tribunes had any notion that Caesar would have them "put to silence" (I ii 295) for removing from his statues the decorations honoring him? Explain.

[*I ii*]

1. Remember that in Shakespeare the scene and act divisions are not to be taken as breaks in the action, with a curtain being drawn and idle chatter starting up in the audience. Each scene flows immediately into the next, and the opening words of any scene should be read or heard with the echo of the preceding ones in mind. How does the opening of scene ii bear out what Flavius has just said? How does it contrast with the clattering exchanges between the tribunes and the crowd?

2. The introduction comments on Caesar's public parading of his wife's barrenness. What other qualities of the man are revealed in this first display of him in action? What significance are we to see in the fact that Caesar refers to himself in the third person? What more do we learn of him through the episode of the Soothsayer's warning? Why does no one pay much attention to the warning? To what is that fact meant to alert us?

3. Why does Brutus remain behind while the rest of the procession moves on? Why does Cassius remain with him? How are we kept reminded of Caesar and the crowd offstage during

their dialogue? How do these reminders affect their dialogue?
(Each time the noise of the crowd is heard, Cassius's addresses to Brutus move to a new tone and subject matter.
Describe these changes in a brief written paragraph.) How
would the effect be altered if Shakespeare had decided to
show us, first, Caesar in the Forum being offered the crown,
and then, separately, Brutus and Cassius in conversation?
Why in your opinion does he *not* show us the Forum scene
directly?

4. The dialogue reveals much about each man and about each
man's attitude toward Caesar (and the reasons for that
attitude):

(a) Why is it significant that Cassius's calculated, if gentle,
chiding of Brutus (36-40) about the coolness of late in
Brutus's "show of love" toward his friend brings forth an
admission that he (Brutus) is "with himself at war" (51) and
therefore withdrawn and neglectful of his friends? He does
not say what is bothering him, but what is suggested?

(b) By what techniques does Cassius feel out Brutus and
prepare him for a direct appeal to join the conspirators: in
lines 60-69? 74-86? 100-41? 145-71? 186-87?

(c) Cassius does most of the talking in the dialogue. Characterize him from what he says and how he says it. How does
he reveal himself to be a man who is "groaning underneath
this age's yoke," as he puts it in line 68?

(d) Characterize Brutus as he reveals himself in his response
to Cassius's heated denunciation of Caesar. How do his references to the shouting in the Forum reveal that he is thinking
about what Cassius is saying more than his guarded replies
might indicate?

(e) Show that, in a sense, Cassius is talking as much to himself, and of himself, as he is taking to, and of, Brutus. Why
does he want, in the words of Flavius earlier, "these growing
feathers plucked from Caesar's wing" (I i 73)? When he
speaks of Brutus's "name" (152-57), could "Cassius" be sub-
stituted just as well?

5. What is the dramatic purpose of Caesar's re-entrance, still
leading the procession? What is his mood? How does it differ
from that we saw in him at the scene's beginning? What may
we infer about his mood from his comments on Cassius?
Would you say that his analysis of Cassius was mostly right
or mostly wrong? In talking to Brutus, Cassius has insisted
that Caesar is both man and symbol. Where in his conversation with Antony (202-26) do these two aspects of Caesar

show themselves? Which of these two aspects was mainly visible in his address to Calphurnia (I ii 1-11)? in his behavior with the Soothsayer (I ii 18-28)? What light does this dualism in Caesar throw on Brutus's problem in II i?

6. The fourth episode in this scene is quite different in tone from the other three. Explain what makes the difference. How does Casca here seem different from the Casca who cried out "Peace, ho! Caesar speaks" at the beginning of the scene? As already noted, we do not see the triple offering of the crown to Caesar; we only hear Casca's flippant and mocking description of it. How would you, as director, handle Caesar's two appearances in conjunction with this incident: as a straightforward display of dignified and awesome leadership? as a display of pompous and self-satisfied showoffery? as a mixture of the two? as something else? Discuss the structure of scene ii considering these questions.

7. Notice that in lines 179-80 Brutus tells Cassius that he will "find a time/Both meet to hear and answer such high things," but that after Casca has finished commenting on the crownofferings, he names a specific time for such a discussion: "To-morrow"(314). What has brought about the change? Show how Cassius has cleverly underlined for his own purposes the implications of Casca's account by his comments during it.

8. What insights into Brutus and Cassius do we get from Cassius's soliloquy (318-32)? Just before Brutus leaves, Cassius tells him to "think of the world." How does his soliloquy show that he is now certain that Brutus will do just that? Cassius has worked hard to land his man. In what manner should he deliver his soliloquy: gloatingly? smugly? cynically? matter-of-factly? how?

[*I iii*]

1. Quite clearly the storm is an integral part of this scene. Given the various reactions to it—and the comments made about it —what is its dramatic function? Consider the scenes that precede and follow it.

2. What do you make of the change in Casca? In the previous episode he was mocking and cynical, using language that was both coarse and blunt. Here there is none of the cynic and his descriptions of the storm and the weird occurrences are lyrical in comparison with his previous speeches. He says to Cicero, "Are you not moved?" Surely he himself is. Why will it be easy for Cassius to land this man too? How does he use

Casca's fear and amazement and his contempt for the "tag-rag people" (I ii 268) to bind him to the conspiracy? Why would he be unable to land a man like Cicero, as he is shown in this scene?
3. Why do all the conspirators feel that they must have Brutus with them if they are going to carry out the conspiracy successfully? Why is it ironic for Casca to say what he says in lines 167-70?

[*II i*]

1. A month of historical time has passed since the Lupercalia when Cassius first talked to Brutus about Caesar's "ambition," but in the movement of the play historical time is of little relevance. Dramatically, this scene follows directly upon the preceding one, which showed the conspiracy hatching on a dark and violent night. It is still night and a sleepless Brutus ("Since Cassius first did whet me against Caesar,/I have not slept" [61-62]) reveals his decision to be part of the conspiracy. How does his language in lines 10-34, 44-58, and 61-69 differ from that of Cassius in the preceding scene? What arguments does he give for joining in the assassination attempt? It has been said that sound personal observations contend here with sound general propositions about the effects of power. Point to the play of these two elements in the speech, and suggest why you think the latter prevails. What would you have decided? Why?
2. Why can't Brutus sleep? Why doesn't he question the sources of the anonymous notes instead of responding to their contents? What really is bothering him in lines 61-69? His vanity has been manipulated by Cassius, as we have seen, but he is also subject to other forces that appeal to his sense of duty, and to his personal integrity, and help him blind himself to himself. Pick out evidences of these forces in his words and actions throughout the scene.
3. How do Brutus's remarks about hiding conspiracy in "smiles and affability" (85) illustrate the corrosion that has already set in upon his character? What is appealing and attractive in his remarks in lines 169-90? What in them is self-deluding and even horrible? Compare the fine distinctions he makes about murder with the great lengths he goes to just before in insisting that oaths are the lot of "priests and cowards and cautelous men." Why, in addition, does he say about Cicero, "O, name him not! Let us not break with him"?

4. What are Brutus's reasons for not including Antony in the assassination attempt? What factors does Cassius take account of that Brutus ignores? Why does he let Brutus's opinion carry the day? In what sense is Trebonius's inane comment (198-99) tragically ironic?

5. Lines 240-44 echo the opening lines of the scene. Why are they significant? How does Lucius's ability to sleep soundly comment on the turmoil in Brutus? Is it only boys who can sleep soundly? Explain.

6. What is the purpose of the scene with Portia at this point? Why is it significant that Brutus has not confided in her at all? There is no doubt about the closeness of the bond between them. What has happened to the peace and calm of their private world? At the moment when her justified reproaches have touched him deeply ("O ye gods,/Render me worthy of this noble wife!"—lines 316-17) a knock from outside is heard. Why is this significant? What other outside "knocks" (verbal and symbolic) have intruded upon Brutus's private garden in this scene? How are they all alike?

7. What further comment is made on the private-public split within Brutus in the brief episode between him and Caius Ligarius? How do Ligarius's words in this episode echo things said by and about Brutus previously?

[*II ii*]

1. In what respects does the scene between Caesar and Calphurnia resemble that between Brutus and Portia? In what respects do the two scenes contrast? How is the relation between the former pair different from that between the latter? How the same? Does the scene between Brutus and Portia make him seem less or more attractive to us? What about the scene between Caesar and Calphurnia in this respect?

2. How much weight does Caesar give to his wife's forebodings? Why does he have the priests "do present sacrifice" if he is so contemptuous of signs and omens? On what grounds does he say finally that he will stay home? How do Calphurnia's misgivings throw light on her husband's haughty dismissal of supernatural warnings? Remember that she has said (14-15), "Caesar, I never stood on ceremonies [gave any thought to omens],/Yet now they fright me."

3. Caesar is the public man par excellence. His use of the third person in referring to himself underscores his awareness of that fact. What other indications of his sense of his public

importance are there in this scene? How well does Decius
know his man in the next episode? How does he break down
Caesar's resolve to stay home from the Senate? (Caesar
blames his wife for the initial decision, even though he also
says, "The cause is in my will: I will not come" [line 76].
Where else has he put Calphurnia in a bad light?)

4. What is the dramatic effect of having the conspirators gather
at Caesar's home to escort him to the Senate House? Has
Caesar done anything yet in the play unescorted, not at the
head of the pack? Characterize Caesar's attitude toward those
who come for him, and theirs toward him. How necessary are
the asides by Trebonius and Brutus in giving ironic impact
to the sharing of the wine ("the sacrament of hospitality and
trust," as Granville-Barker calls it)? Contrast their asides with
Caesar's open words in between (134-35).

5. The storm and the accompanying unnatural events remain
more than simply background noise and confusion appropri-
ate to the horror of the impending murder. Compare Casca's
account in I iii with Calphurnia's in this scene. For instance,
what kinds of unnatural events are reported? How do they
underscore and thus make more terrible the "natural" human
actions that are unfolding?

6. As the group prepares to share some wine before going to
the Senate House, the moment is at hand for the final shattering of Caesar's public world and Brutus's private world in
the murder in the Capitol. To appreciate the full tragic significance of this shattering, it is necessary to believe in the
"greatness" of Caesar despite his human flaws, in the pre-
eminence of Brutus's integrity, honor, and gentleness, despite
*his* flaws, and in the genuineness of their love for each other
and for Rome. Were Caesar simply a clever and ruthless
leader, or Brutus a sham paragon, or their love a convenient
public display, then the whole proceeding would be a blood-
letting of interest only to those who like to witness atrocities.
How you weigh the merits of each "side" in the confronta-
tion that develops will depend to a great extent on what you
think the possibilities are of living by "principles" both privately and publicly. Try to put in writing how you see both
Caesar and Brutus at this stage of the play. Support your
statements with specific references to the evidence provided
by the play. Where has Shakespeare labored to make Brutus
appealing? unappealing? Where has he labored to make
Caesar appealing? unappealing? Some comments on Cassius
might also be in order.

[*II iii and iv*]

Scenes iii and iv serve a single purpose. In the movement of the play they prepare for the powerful beginning of Act III as the Soothsayer and Artemidorus attempt to warn Caesar. What makes them wish to warn him? Who else knows what will happen and yet cannot change the course of events? Why is it dramatically important to have these three quite different people aware of what is planned and yet equally unable to do anything about it?

[*III i*]

1. How do the opening lines of the scene underscore ironically the strengths and weaknesses of both Caesar and the conspirators? Consider:

(a) The Soothsayer counters Caesar's opening arrogant comment beautifully, but Caesar ignores him and that is the end of him and his warning. Artemidorus tries to tell Caesar that his suit "touches Caesar nearer," but (all the more because he is always on display) the great man immediately—and predictably—puts himself last, so the warning gets a result opposite from what was intended, and Artemidorus is gone from the action and the play.

(b) Why is Cassius's remark (12-13) wryly amusing?

(c) Lines 14-33 show the conspirators maneuvering for position. What is the purpose of Popilius's comment? How is Brutus revealed as truly the leader of the conspiracy now? How does the language of the lines reveal the anxiety and tension in all the conspirators except Brutus? What do these considerations show about how we are to regard him?

(d) Why are Caesar's words in lines 34-35 almost unbearably ironic? What kind of activity does "Are we all ready?" suggest? What does "amiss" mean? Does planned murder suggest that things are "amiss"? Who is it that "must redress" things that are "amiss"? Caesar and *his* Senate, no less! In Brutus's mouth the questions under the circumstances would ring naively enough. In what cosmic sense is Caesar, too, naive?

2. The introduction notes that the surrounding of Caesar by the conspirators must be seen—and handled on stage—with "a coloring of priest-like ritual." How does the language show that "one by one [the conspirators] kneel before this demigod"? How do Caesar's words from line 34 ("Are we all ready?") to line 80 ("Hence! Wilt thou lift up Olympus?") reveal that he sees himself as godlike, even if he would deny

it? Point out the phrases that mark his attitude unmistakably.
Does it make any difference in the meaning of the episode
whether Metellus Cimber's suit is just or not? Explain.

3. All through the scene Caesar is totally and arrogantly his public self, in sharp contrast with his behavior toward the same
men just before leaving for the Senate House. What is Shakespeare's purpose in showing this duality in the man? How
does this treatment make his final, private words, "Et tu,
Brutè? Then fall Caesar," immeasurably more ironic in relation to both himself and Brutus than simply a close friendship
would suggest?

4. The assassination attempt is surprisingly successful. How do
the conspirators react to that success? The shouts of "liberty"
and "freedom" do not ring hollowly at first: the conspirators'
minds and words are all on Rome, they seek no further
killing, and they are ready to die defending the rightness of
what they have done. It is not until Casca's fatuous comment
in lines 111-12, topped by Brutus's even more fatuous extension of it, that we are struck by the enormity of the bloody
act. At that very point, how does the return of "ceremonial"
action through Brutus's suggestion (115-20) drive home with
savage effect the irony of his own echoing words: "Let's all
cry 'Peace, freedom, and liberty!' "? Show how the following
declamations by Cassius, and then Brutus, and then Cassius
again pile ironic horror on horror, even while the speakers
remain wholly oblivious of what they are really saying. What
in your view are they "really saying"?

5. The conspirators prepare to leave for their own triumphal
procession through Rome, with Brutus in the lead à la Caesar
and "the most boldest and best hearts of Rome" at "his heels"
(133). At that very moment, the counterconspiracy begins
with the arrival of Antony's servant, who re-enacts the ceremonial kneeling of the conspirators around Caesar. What is
the import and tone of the words Antony's mouthpiece
speaks? What do they tell us of Antony? Up until now, have
there been any suggestions, by word or deed, that Antony
will prove to be the antagonist he does prove to be? Discuss.

6. How do the two speeches referred to immediately above, and
lines 198-225 and 243-47, indicate that Antony is a master
dissembler, that he knows how to handle men like Brutus,
and that he is already preparing his counterthrust? Consider
the mixture of praise and rebuke he heaps on the conspirators
(rebuke in what form?); the repeating of the blood ceremony
but in different form (how does he cleverly destroy the

"knot" idea suggested by Cassius [127-29]); the kinds of images he uses to characterize the murder; and the double meanings throughout.

7. Why does Brutus fall so easily for Antony's dissembling? How is his treatment of Antony consistent with his earlier attempts to put the assassination on a high moral plane? How do his comments in lines 239-42 mock his professed moral integrity? How does Cassius by contrast, even though he says little in the episode, further underscore the practical and moral blindness of Brutus?

8. What does Antony's soliloquy (274-95) show us about future developments? We already know how he feels about the murder, and we are sure that he will not befriend the conspirators. Consider the language of his prophecy of what the future holds. Consider also the dramatic effect of having him speak thus to Caesar's body. In what sense is Caesar not dead? Some commentators have said that Caesar has a static, relatively unimportant role in the play. Show that this is not so, that, in a sense, he is more important—even more active—dead than alive, and that Antony is well aware of that fact.

9. What purposes are served by the last episode? What characteristics of Antony are underlined (note particularly lines 302-5)? Why is Octavius important? (Notice that Caesar has sent for him.) Why is it dramatically effective (and also necessary on the Elizabethan stage) to have Caesar's body carried off to "the marketplace" by Antony and Octavius's servant? What does the servant's reaction at line 301 allow us to foresee?

[*III ii*]

1. While Antony and the servant are en route to the Forum with Caesar's body, Brutus and the other conspirators have arrived there to "satisfy" the plebeians. Once again the crowd takes a central role in the play, first responding to Brutus, then to Antony, and then to Cinna the Poet in a bloody, senseless climax that shows what a mob can be—in republican Rome or anywhere else. In the dramatic flow of the play the crowd must be seen as "acting" as well as "acted upon." How does Brutus treat them?

2. His speech has been variously viewed. Some have said that it is well put together rhetorically but too abstract in its argument to be followed. Others have called it a great speech, appealing, as one would expect in Brutus's case, to principles

and ideas that the crowd has little grasp of and no interest in. Which of these views, or mixture of them, do you uphold? Why?

3. Eventually Brutus prevails with the crowd. Judging from their spoken comments, what would you say they are persuaded by? Why does he fail to take advantage of his victory? What qualities in him are brought out by his going out alone and urging the crowd to stay and hear Antony?

4. How does Antony treat the same plebeians? It has been said that Brutus, in *his* oration, talks only to himself; Antony, in his, to the people as they are. What is meant by this? How many indications of what Antony's approach will be can you detect in his first words (80-81)? Analyze his speech. What did the critic mean who said that in a school for rabble-rousers, Antony's oration should be the whole curriculum? What elements do you find here that are likely to be found always in speeches designed to rouse the emotions of large numbers of people? What specific appeals does Antony make to the feelings of sympathy and pity? What appeal to curiosity? What appeal to greed? Why does he re-enact the assassination? Since he did not witness it, how do you account for such lines as 181-96? Antony mentions the will in line 135, but does not read it until line 249. Why not?

5. Characterize Antony in this scene. The speech and his gloating dismissal of responsibility, "Mischief, thou art afoot,/ Take thou what course thou wilt" (268-69) suggest a devious, cool-headed riot-inciter, but there is more to him than that. Put his behavior here in the balance with his reasons for so behaving.

6. What is the purpose of the brief episode at the close of scene ii?

[III iii]

What is the significance of this final scene of the mob in action? How many different kinds of senseless behavior occur, culminating in the inhuman tearing to pieces of an innocent man simply because he has the same name as one of the conspirators? What mass-scale chaos is foreshadowed in the brutality of this episode? Who is responsible for such chaos? Explain. What does the cruel dismembering of the poor poet have to say about the hacking down of "mighty Caesar"?

[*IV i*]

1. How do the opening lines of the scene repeat on the private level the senseless and bloody public behavior that closed Act III? (Some time has obviously elapsed since the close of Act III, but there is no sense of time lapse and the meeting of these three men has been prepared for by the concluding episode of III ii.) Characterize Antony as he is shown here. Do the same for Octavius. The latter will have increasing importance in the play. Antony is still in control, but what suggestions are there that Octavius is an even better opportunist? What is the purpose of the long discussion of Lepidus? What differences of personality do Octavius and Antony show in the course of it?
2. How does the scene prepare for the scene to come?

[*IV ii*]

The last two acts take place in the heart of civil war, a fit setting for the chaos let loose by the assassination. In scene i Anthony says that Brutus and Cassius are "levying powers"; in scenes ii and iii we see the two with their powers, but not themselves, fully prepared for battle. What purposes are served in scene ii? Do the two meet to coordinate plans or for some other reasons? Explain. What hints of change do we see in each man?

[*IV iii*]

1. There is no real break in the action between scenes ii and iii. The first words between the two men had been blunt, almost discourteous. The quarrel proceeds in the same vein inside Brutus's tent. Granville-Barker says that the scene is "dominated by Brutus and attuned in the main to his mood." How is this comment borne out in the quarrel? What faults does Brutus find in Cassius? Does Cassius defend himself or make excuses? What faults does Cassius find in Brutus? How does Brutus reply? How do both men reveal the same strengths and weaknesses each has shown before? What dramatic purposes does this long quarrel serve? Consider how many kinds of "disorder" have been shown since the murder of Caesar.
2. Contrast the manner and substance of the quarrel between Brutus and Cassius with the manner and substance of the disagreements (spoken and unspoken) in scene i. The quarrel scene comes on the heels of the cold-blooded ticking off of those scheduled for slaughter and the thinly veiled hint that

one of the trio of rulers will not last long. In contrast, the quarrel explodes dramatically, and we are not at all sure that blood won't flow. If there can be a preference for displays of contention, potentially violent, where do your sympathies lie as between the two episodes and why? Consider also how each "contention" is finally ended.

3. Brutus and Cassius recall themselves to themselves before the poet breaks in and before Brutus reveals Portia's suicide. Why is the timing significant? Why hasn't Brutus mentioned the suicide previously?

4. In a variety of ways in this scene Brutus is shown in command of himself and of the forces opposed to Antony and Octavius. We have already looked at the quarrel episode. What further ways does Shakespeare use to center the dramatic action on him and for what dramatic purposes?

(a) Consider his overriding Cassius's advice about battle plans. What reasons does he give for having things his way? Where else has he overridden Cassius to their disadvantage?

(b) What is underscored about Brutus in his attitude toward Lucius? toward Varro and Claudius? Why is it significant that the three can go to sleep so easily and that Brutus remains awake?

(c) What purpose is served by the appearance of the ghost? It is Caesar's ghost all right, not some "weakness in mine eyes," as Brutus says; but in what sense is it also Brutus's "evil spirit," as the ghost calls itself? Brutus takes the appearance calmly, but what is ominous about it? Why did it appear? Remember that Brutus had only moments before decided to march to Philippi.

(d) Why does he wake the sleeping men? What is dramatically effective about the close of the scene and the act?

[V]

1. What was said before about act and scene divisions is especially true for Act V. The act must be treated as one continuous flow, bringing the inner private battle in Brutus to an external climax on the public battlefield of Philippi. What change has by now taken place in the relationship between Antony and Octavius? What is the purpose of the virulent exchange between the four generals? Who has the better of it, if anyone? How does this exchange illustrate the soliloquy by Antony at the close of III i (274-95)?

2. Do the words of Cassius to Messala and the dialogue between him and Brutus mock the brave show of their exchange with Antony and Octavius? If not, what do you make of this episode, which Granville-Barker calls, "a chill, quiet talk." If defeat is in their hearts, and if both of them know it, does that make them cowards—or something else? Discuss.

3. What is the purpose of scene ii, opening on an emptied stage after the ominous, repeated "farewells" between Brutus and Cassius? What is the effect of the alarum just before Brutus and Messala burst on stage? What Brutus have we here?

4. We next switch to Cassius, as fully in command of himself at this opening moment as Brutus, but getting the worst of the battle with Antony. He soon gets two false reports (one by Titinius in lines 5-8 and one by Pindarus in lines 29-33) and precipitously, foolishly, makes no attempt to check either. Why is his response uncharacteristic of the man? In what ways does his death foreshadow Brutus's, which is soon to come?

5. The business of having Young Cato "proclaim [his] name" only to have it silenced and of Lucilius pretending to be Brutus and thus unintentionally saving his neck (because of Antony's generosity!) provides the dying gasp for conspiracy. Show how the double bit of bravado prepares dramatically, by contrast, for the last episode, which begins on the most sober of notes ("Come, poor remains of friends, rest on this rock" [V v 1]) and proceeds quickly to a close, punctuated by the alarums from outside.

6. What is the final picture we get of Brutus? How do his followers see him? How does he treat his servant Strato and get treated in turn? What do his last words, "Caesar, now be still,/I killed not thee with half so good a will," mean? Why are they more revealing of his essential nobility than Antony's "sportsmanlike" gesture of farewell or Octavius's polite and proper comments, however true? How also do those very words drive harshly home the tragic irony of the play? (He means them with a depth and sincerity that Antony and Octavius could never understand.)

7. Who has the last words in the play? How do we know that he is now running the show? What does he say and do? How would Brutus or Cassius like the Rome that Octavius will rule? From what we have seen of Octavius in the play, would you say that it would be a better Rome than Julius Caesar's or worse? In what respects?

# SHAKESPEARE AND HIS WORKS

*i*

William Shakespeare was born in the Warwickshire town of Stratford on April 23, 1564 (a guess based on the record of his baptism dated April 26) and died there on April 23, 1616. He was the eldest of six children of John and Mary (Arden) Shakespeare. His father was a successful glovemaker and trader in Stratford and for a time was active in local civic and political affairs, serving for a term as high bailiff, or chief administrative officer of the town; his mother was the daughter of a prosperous landowner. At age 18 he married Anne Hathaway, a woman some eight years his senior, by whom he had three children, Susanne in 1583, Hamnet and Judith (twins) in 1585.

Although he obviously spent most of his time in London between 1585 and 1611, he kept close ties with his home town, and his own family lived there throughout most of the year. In 1597 he purchased New Place, one of Stratford's finest homes, to which he retired in 1611.

There is no record of his formal schooling, but he undoubtedly attended the Stratford grammar school and got a solid grounding in Latin and literature since the masters during his school age years were Oxford graduates. When or why he went to London and turned to acting and writing plays is not known, but by 1592 he had clearly established a reputation in both fields; and for the next twenty years he turned out an average of almost two plays a year, plus a number of sonnets and several longer poems. He was a charter member of the Lord Chamberlain's Men, an acting company formed in 1594 (renamed the

King's Men in 1603), the foremost company of its time. He remained with the King's Men until his retirement. In 1599 the company moved into the newly built Globe Theater, in which Shakespeare had a financial interest. By that time, and for the rest of his life, he prospered financially through his acting-writing-investing ventures. More important, in his own time he was a widely respected and widely loved dramatist in an age that produced many and for an audience that understood and supported the theater.

*ii*

A chronological listing of Shakespeare's published works follows. There is no certainty about most of the assigned dates, and probably never will be. As we have indicated in the Textual Note, there was in Shakespeare's day little of the concern we have for the printing of play scripts, and most of the assigned dates for composition are the result of scholarly research and supposition based on both external and internal evidence that we here need only to recognize.

**PLAYS**

| | |
|---|---|
| 1588–93 | *The Comedy of Errors* |
| 1588–94 | *Love's Labor's Lost* |
| 1590–91 | *2 Henry VI* |
| 1590–91 | *3 Henry VI* |
| 1591–92 | *1 Henry VI* |
| 1592–93 | *Richard III* |
| 1592–94 | *Titus Andronicus* |
| 1593–94 | *The Taming of the Shrew* |
| 1593–95 | *The Two Gentlemen of Verona* |
| 1594–96 | *Romeo and Juliet* |
| 1595 | *Richard II* |
| 1594–96 | *A Midsummer Night's Dream* |
| 1596–97 | *King John* |
| 1596–97 | *The Merchant of Venice* |
| 1597 | *1 Henry IV* |
| 1597–98 | *2 Henry IV* |
| 1598-1600 | *Much Ado About Nothing* |
| 1598–99 | *Henry V* |

| 1599 | *Julius Caesar* |
| 1599–1600 | *As You Like It* |
| 1599–1600 | *Twelfth Night* |
| 1600–1601 | *Hamlet* |
| 1597–1601 | *The Merry Wives of Windsor* |
| 1601–2 | *Troilus and Cressida* |
| 1602–4 | *All's Well That Ends Well* |
| 1603–4 | *Othello* |
| 1604 | *Measure for Measure* |
| 1605–6 | *King Lear* |
| 1605–6 | *Macbeth* |
| 1606–7 | *Antony and Cleopatra* |
| 1605–8 | *Timon of Athens* |
| 1607–9 | *Coriolanus* |
| 1608–9 | *Pericles* |
| 1609–10 | *Cymbeline* |
| 1610–11 | *The Winter's Tale* |
| 1611 | *The Tempest* |
| 1612–13 | *Henry VIII* |

### POEMS

| 1592 | *Venus and Adonis* |
| 1593–94 | *The Rape of Lucrece* |
| 1593–1600 | *Sonnets* |
| 1600–1601 | *The Phoenix and the Turtle* |

# BOOKS, RECORDS, FILMS

Further reading about Shakespeare's times, his theater, and the plays themselves is always valuable and enlightening. Suggested below is a short list of excellent books, most of which are in print in inexpensive editions. Also included is information about available recordings of the complete text of *Julius Caesar* and about 16mm films for rental.

*Books*

(Books marked with an asterisk are available in inexpensive editions.)

* Bentley, Gerald E. *Shakespeare: A Biographical Handbook.* New Haven: Yale University Press.

Campbell, O. J., and Edward G. Quinn. *The Reader's Encyclopedia of Shakespeare.* New York: Thomas Y. Crowell.

Chambers, E. K. *William Shakespeare: A Study of Facts and Problems.* 2 vols. London: Oxford University Press.

* Dean, Leonard F. (ed.). *Shakespeare: Modern Essays in Criticism.* New York: Oxford University Press.

* Granville-Barker, Harley. *Prefaces to Shakespeare.* Vol. II. Princeton: Princeton University Press.

* Harbage, Alfred. *Shakespeare's Audience.* New York: Columbia University Press.

* Kernan, Alvin B. (ed.). *Modern Shakespearean Criticism.* New York: Harcourt Brace Jovanovich, Inc.

* Nagler, A. M. *Shakespeare's Stage.* tr. by Ralph Manheim. New Haven: Yale University Press.

*Recordings*

(All recordings are released in both monaural and stereo; the text will differ in minor respects from that used in this edition.)

1. Shakespeare Recording Society (Caedmon Records). Ralph Richardson, Anthony Quayle, John Mills. 3 12-in. records. Also available on tape.
2. The Marlowe Society. 3 12-in. records.
3. The Dublin Gate Players. 3 12-in. records.

*Films*

1. 1950. David Bradley, Charlton Heston. 90 minutes. 16mm sound, black and white. Rent from Audio Film Center, Crowell Collier Macmillan, 866 Third Avenue, New York, NY 10022.
2. 1953. Marlon Brando, James Mason. 121 minutes. 16mm sound, black and white. Rent from Films, Inc., 4420 Oakton St., Skokie, Ill. 60076.
3. BBC. 120 minutes. 16mm sound, black and white. Rent from Time-Life Films, 43 W. 16th St., New York, NY 10011.